DINGLE FOLK TALES

LUKE EASTWOOD

Illustrated by Elena Danaan

electric publications

Never let the truth get in the way of a good story.
Mark Twain

Dedicated to the memory of Hugh Brennan,
a good friend and a great storyteller, if ever there was one.

By the same author:

Where The Hazel Falls (Editor)

The Druid's Primer

The Journey

Through The Cracks In The Concrete The Wilderness Grows

Kerry Folk Tales (with Gary Branigan)

How To Save The Planet

The Druid Garden

Samhain: The Roots of Halloween

Articles: lukeeastwood.com

First Published by Electric Publications, 2022

Electric Publications, Co. Kerry, Ireland
www.electricpublications.com

Paperback ISBN: 978-1-7398625-0-3
EBook ISBN: 978-1-7398625-1-0

Edited, designed, printed and bound, on 100% recycled paper,
in the Republic of Ireland

Printed by Modern Printers, Kilkenny, Ireland
modernprinters.ie

Contents

Acknowledgements

I'd like to thank all those who helped me in the creation of this book, especially Elena Danaan and Bob Ó Cathail, for their wonderful illustration work. I'd also like to thank all those who offered help, made suggestions and gave inspirational ideas, such as Sophie Murphy, Br. John Aherne, John Knox, Eimear Burke, Kathleen O'Sullivan, Rob Lowther and Seán Brosnan. I'd also like to thank the people I interviewed – Martin Knightly, Catherine Merrigan, Adrian Fitzgerald, John Francis Brosnan, Jerry Bácaéir, Timothy Murphy, Marie Lenihan and Áine Uí Dhúbhsláine for their generosity and time. Thanks to Dúchas, The Schools' Collection, New Island Books (for permission to use a Peig Sayers story) and thanks also to Dingle Library for their treasure trove of books, that I had access to, and for the kind help of the library staff. Finally a big thank you to Cyril Harrington for help with translation into English and to John Knox for proof-reading and continuity checks.

Introduction

I first visited Dingle town in 2006, with my mother and my daughter on a particularly damp and horrible day. We didn't stay that long and we departed towards Tralee via the famous Connor Pass (*An Chonair*), of which we saw almost nothing, on account of the heavy mist. Several years later I returned to Dingle and I eventually moved here in 2015. Since that second visit, I managed to get a good look at the Connor Pass, on one of the relatively rare sunny days, and I realised how truly stunning it is.

Over time I've had the pleasure to traverse the entire peninsula by car and on foot, in various weather conditions - needless to say with a good coat, sturdy boots and a hat in tow, even in the middle of summer. I've been lucky to be invited to events that few non-residents ever see, such as the St John's Eve bonfire and musical evenings in houses perched on the edge of the eastern Atlantic ocean. I have even celebrated Burns Night (a Scottish tradition), during a power outage, eating haggis by candlelight to the accompaniment of song and laughter.

This peninsula is unique, as are all the western peninsulas of Kerry and Cork, each having their own charm. Dingle is a small peninsula but it is rammed full of interesting historical artifacts - one can barely travel anywhere without running into an ancient monument, dwelling, castle, church or ring-fort. It is also the subject of countless stories, some of which are local variants of well-known Irish tales and others which are particular to just this part of the world.

Dingle and its hinterland is one of the most well-known and popular *Gaeltacht* (Irish speaking) areas, and one that has also produced a huge number of both native speaking and English speaking writers, including the infamous *gaeilgeoir* Peig Sayers (much hated by many school children), of the Blasket Islands.

The stories presented here are culled from many different sources and span a vast quantity of time – from the unrecorded prehistory of this area, up to modern day, many related to me by people who are still very much alive today.

There are so many stories that one might choose from that this book could conceivably have been twice or even three times as long as it actually is. However, it would take a great many years to collect and retell the hundreds of stories that are held in the old books and the memories of the local people - what I offer here is just a small sample of the treasure trove that exists.

Particularly as I am a total 'blow in', it has been an honour to retell some of the stories of *Corca Dhuibhne*, some of which are known to many, but many of which are largely forgotten, particularly outside of west Kerry. It is a great privilege to be able to collect these stories together and pass them on for future generations to enjoy and hopefully preserve. May the stories of the Dingle Peninsula and the art of storytelling never be forgotten!

Luke Eastwood, Dingle, December 2021.

Dingle - The Story of a Name

It is suggested that Kerry has been inhabited since about 5000 BCE and there is evidence of early inhabitants all across the Dingle Peninsula (*Corca Dhuibhne*), in the form of the ancient stone monuments scattered all over it. Even in and around the town of Dingle there is still evidence of this distant habitation – the buluan stone (known as the holy stone) on the roadside at upper main street, with its six cup indentations. Just outside the town, in Milltown are two significant standing stones (the gates of glory), a recumbant stone covered in rock art (perhaps from 2000 BCE) and near by another large megaltith.

On the way to Lispole there are a multitude of stone ring forts, a ring of ogham stones, standing stones (*gallán*) and ancient stone alignments, such as at *Arda Mór* Upper and Lower. On the other side of the Connor Pass a line of 5 stones (2 fallen) marks the equinoxes and standing stones, raths, beehive huts and remains of huts continue all the way to the end of the peninsula where it meets the *Sliabh Mis* mountains. Going back the other way (Back West) there are a plethora of megalithic, bronze age and iron age sites, in fact one can hardly travel a mile in any direction without almost tripping over some ancient monument!

So we can see that the Dingle Peninsula, stretching about 30 miles out into the Atlantic, has a history that slips way back into the mists of time, long before writing and recorded history was of any concern. What we do have though, is a rich oral history of the area, the places and the names and folklore surrounding them, much of which has long ago been written down, while some of it currently still has not.

Corca Dhuibne, the name given to the whole peninsula, was anglicized as Corkaguiny, which became the name of the baronry, prior to Irish independence. The name roughly translates as the 'tribe of Duibhne', reputed to be an ancient Celtic goddess, who may be an alternative name of Dovinia, a goddess name that appears on at least 2 ogham stones on the peninsula. The people (*túath*) of *Dhuibhne* once occupied the peninsula in the bronze age, and perhaps into the early middle ages (also possessing territories in the south and east of Kerry), gave their name to the peninsula, still used to this day.

The town itself is named in English as a corruption and shortening of the Irish *Daingean Uí Chúis. Daingean* means fortress in English but *Chúis* is a name, thought to be derived from the Norman name De La Cousa, first mentioned by a chronicler during the reign of Elizabeth I of England - Sir Nicholas White, in 1580. However, there are two other derivations of the name- one being the Gaelic chieftan *Ó Cúis*, who ruled the area prior to the Norman invasion. The other alternative is that *Cúis* refers to the Hussey family, another Norman name, but one that became *Ó hEoghusa* through integration into Gaelic society over time. In the Dingle area, the name dropped the 'O' - spelled Husae. The Husseys certainly played a colourful role in the history of the town, as early as 1307. We do not know which explanation is correct, with many favouring the *Ó Cúis* chieftan, although there is no mention of any such line in any of the pre-Norman Irish annals. So here we are, with 3 possible sources of the name *Daingean Uí Chúis*, but with no conclusive evidence to substantiate any of them!

Ancient Forts/Raths

Corca Dhuibhne, the Dingle Peninsula has one of the highest concentrations of ringforts or raths in the country. The tradition of leaving these forts untouched, and to the fairies, is still very much alive to this day. One can find a fine collection of forts in various states of repair all across the peninsula. Some are repaired and restored to what they may have once looked like, while others are left entirely to nature and often completely overgrown. A common theme is that many of these forts are homes to ghosts, strange apparitions, fairies or *Tuatha Dé Danann* (the Sidhe) and so it is often considered best to let sleeping dogs lie!

There are many stories associated with ancient raths, some of which were built in the Christian era, but many of which date back thousands of years. These few stories were collected from the Camp area, on the north side of the peninsula, but each local area has its own unique stories, history and legends.

*

There is a fort (*rath*) in Glendine. It is called *Lios an Garsúinín Dubh* and this is because the ghost of a little black boy used to come out of it by night and go down to the field called *Páirc an Garsúinín Dubh* and stop there by night and he would return up to the fort again in the morning as the sun rose.

There is another old fort in *Curra Cuillneach* called *Lios na Broc* and there is another one called *Lios na Cait (Lios na gCat) mar bíonn cat ann gach oiche. Bíonn cat ann.* One night when one of the Fianna was coming down from the fort a great cat came before him and went in at the lower side and came out at the upper side of the road and he never saw him passing up.

There are two forts in *Curra*, but one of them is called *Lios na h-Amhairce*. Twenty or thirty years ago a woman was going down the road near it, when she heard the milking of cows inside in it. The lady looked across into it and could see no one. The other fort is called *Lios Parcín Rellig*, for long ago people used to get relics there. There is a fort near the old Dingle road called *Lios an Fear Ghranna*. By night there used to be an old whiskery man be seen there, who was no doubt a ghost from times gone by. At *Lios na Damh Deirg* in Knockglas there used to be light seen there at night going from there over to the fort in Joe Dunne's field.

There is a fort in Thomas Murphy's field called *Liosín Bán* and lights do be seen there at night. There is a fort in *Coillín Beag* called where can be found a 'Will-o'-the-Wisp'. Every night there used to be a light seen there and one night as a man was going home a light came before him, putting the fear of God into him!

There is a fort in Tom Dean's field called *Lios a Duinín* because it is in a field called *Gort a Dúna* and long ago music used to be heard there. There is also a fort in James O'Donnell's field called *Lios a Brannair*.

Based on an account collected by Máighréad Ní Dhomhnaill from Tomás Ó Domhnaill (*An Cam*/Camp)

The Last Knights of Kerry and Rathinane Castle

The Knight of Kerry is one of three ancient hereditary knighthoods created by the first Baron Desmond, John Fitzgerald. The other two titles were White Knight and Knight of Glin, although both of these are now extinct. After the death of his first wife, John remarried to Honora, daughter of Hugh O'Connor of Kerry. He had three sons with Honora, who could not inherit his Baronry, which would go to his first son. As a Count Palatine he had the right to create knighthoods for his three younger sons, which were passed on down the generations

The White Knights, established in Limerick and Kilkenny, began with Maurice Fitzgibbon, grandson of Baron Desmond although this knighthood ended in 1611 with the death of the 12th White Knight (another Maurice) who had no children. Although attempts have since been made, unsuccessfully, to claim the title.

The Knights of Glin bore the name Fitzgerald, the first being Sir John Fitz-John Fitzgerald, who built the family's castle on the Shannon estuary in Co. Limerick. Despite a certain rebelliousness, including towards Elizabeth I, the knights continued after the destruction of the castle into the 21st century. The last knight, Desmond Fitzgerald, still lived at the Glin manor, close to the original castle, but died there of cancer in 2011, leaving three daughters and no sons to inherit the title.

The last surviving Irish knight is Adrian Fitzgerald, the current Knight Of Kerry. The Knights Of Kerry once owned

Rahinane (Rathinnane/Rahanane) Castle, built inside an ancient rath, overlooking both Ventry and Dingle bays, the ruins of which can still be seen today. The castle is unusual in that it is built inside a large ringfort, built much earlier in the 7th or 8th century CE, which was originally called Rath Fhionnáin or Finan's ringfort. According to a local legend, this fort and surrounding lands was the last in Ireland held by the Vikings, as it was so highly defensible, with a massively deep and wide ditch. From the creation of the title in the 13th century, Rathinane was the primary residence of the Knights of Kerry, and the existing castle was probably built in the 15th century, although it was destroyed by Cromwell's troops around 1650.

The author was fortunate enough to interview the current owner of Rathinane Castle in 2021, who explained how it came into his family. The castle came into the possession of the 1st Lord Ventry (Sir Thomas Mullins who was made Baron Ventry in 1800). Subsequently the castle and surrounding farmland was given to a Mr Armstrong, a parson and thereafter to a Morris Nelligan (a steward for the Mullins family) in the late 1800s. Nelligan had a wife and three daughters but he died young very unexpectedly and his widow remarried to one Dan Murphy – the great-grandfather of the current owner. The castle passed to Dan's son Tim, then to his grandson Dan and finally to great-grandson and sheep farmer, Timothy Murphy. The Murphys have opened the rath and castle to members of the public during the tourist season, a visit well worth making for those interested in unusual historical places.

From the late 18th century the Knights Of Kerry also resided at Valentia Island. Adrian's ancestor, Sir Peter Fitzgerald 19th Knight of Kerry, was instrumental in the creation of the seaport, railway terminal, the building of Knightstown and the transatlantic cable used for the first Telegraph message sent from America to Europe.

Adrian Fitzgerald, now in his late seventies, is a distant cousin of the last Knight of Glin, Desmond Fitzgerald, who he knew well and considered a friend. Interviewed by a newspaper after Desmond's death, Adrian expressed his sadness at being the last of three Irish Knights. Adrian Fitzgerald was born in Britain in 1940, where his father George was serving as an officer in the army during World War Two. Adrian became a Conservative Party politician and was Mayor of Kensington (in London) in the 1980s. He is retired now and divides his time between London and his estate in County Waterford.

In discussion with the author in 2019, Adrian revealed that reports that he will be the final Knight Of Kerry are incorrect. The Knight of Kerry, a title that has been handed down for over 700 years, will be passed on to the next generation. Like his distant cousin Desmond, Adrian, who is also Baronet of Valencia as well as 24th Knight of Kerry, has no sons. However, Adrian does have an heir, his 3rd cousin Anthony Fitzgerald, who has a son, who should eventually inherit the title after Anthony.

The Haunted Bothereen

A mháthair féin a d'innis an scéal do. Cailleadh í 7 mbliana ó shoin agus bhí sí 70 bl. an uair sin. Ní fheadair sé an mo bliain o chualaidh sé e. Tógadh an bhean san i gCeapach Cloch, An Cam, agus de mhúintir Dhubdha ab'eadh í sin.

There were two roads which would take people into Camp, one was long and the other was a short-cut. One was a bothereen and supposedly haunted and so the local priest said from the altar that no-one should go by that road, between nine o'clock and cock-crow in the morning.

Long ago two men, both riding upon a single horse, were coming home from a fair and they came to the split in the road. The two, after some discussion, said that they would go by the short-cut. When they were a little way up the bothereen, the horse began to shy and they began to feel somewhat nervous.

After a short while they saw a woman dressed in black clothes coming towards them. She said it was very late that they were out and they said it was just as late that she was out. The old woman laughed and then she gave one of the men three pieces of stick and told him that they would meet three dogs and if they (the dogs) would make for them to give them a stick each and that they would pass in safety if they did as instructed.

As expected the two men on the horse met the dogs one after the other. Each dog growled ominously but each time one of the men gave them one of the sticks and so they passed on unharmed. The next person they met on the way home was the parish priest of their place and he accused them of going by the haunted road, without his leave to do so.

The two men confessed that they had come by that way and he asked them if they saw anything, and so they told him their strange story. The priest said it was a good job that he, himself didn't catch up to the old woman. However, the priest must have caught her soon after, for he preached from the altar a few Sundays after that everyone could go by that road again, at any time of the day or the night. Indeed, he said he had sent the old woman to Crumhán Strand making *sugáin* (ropes) of the sand. The name of the road is *Gleann Scoirthín* and three men were found dead there one after the other, the summer after.

Based on a story collected by Nóra Ní Chroidheain from Diarmuid Ó Chroidheain (*An Cam*/Camp)

Tom Crean the Antarctic Explorer of Anascaul

Tom Crean was largely unknown a few decades ago, at least outside of county Kerry, but this unassuming and quiet Kerryman was a major figure in the exploration of Antarctica in the early 1900s.

Crean was born in 1877, near to Anascaul on the Dingle Peninsula, to Catherine and Patrick Crean on their farm at Gurtuchrane. As one of ten children he spent much of his time helping out on the farm, where they mostly grew potatoes and raised cattle. He learned to read and write at school but is thought to have left at age 12 to help his father with the farm. It's been suggested that after an altercation with his father Crean decided to leave and join the British Navy at the earliest opportunity. At 15 he made his way to a Royal Navy station at Minard, lying about his age, he managed to sign up in July of 1893.

Tom, joining as a Boy 2nd class, served on a variety of different warships and proved himself to be hardworking and reliable and was eventually promoted to petty officer, 2nd class before being posted to New Zealand on the torpedo vessel Ringarooma in 1900. In December 1901 the Ringarooma gave assistance to Robert Scott's ship "Discovery".

Crean might well have disappeared into obscurity had not an able seaman, Harry Barker, deserted the Discovery after striking a petty officer and left Scott a man short for his expedition. Twenty four year old Crean, having a reputation for being tough, was accepted by Scott when he volunteered as

Barker's replacement and so began the frozen adventures that would make him famous.

Tom was well liked by his comrades and was considered one of the best at hauling sledges across the ice, which he did for a total of 149 days. Crean was one of twelve men who traveled further south, at that time in 1902, than any humans had done before but he returned to base camp while Scott, Shackleton and Wilson pressed on before being forced to turn back, still some 500 miles from the south pole.

Unfortunately Discovery had become trapped in the ice that winter and even in the summer of 1902-03 they were unable to break free. Crean and most of the crew stayed with the ship, while Shackleton left on a relief ship. During two years stuck in Antarctica Crean survived falling through thin ice and other harsh experiences before Discovery was finally freed in February 1904 and returned to Portsmouth. Scott singled him out for his excellent work and recommended him for promotion to petty officer 1st class.

Scott also requested that Crean, now a valuable and trusted colleague, join him, serving together on several ships over the next few years. Scott also chose Crean as one of the first to join him on his ship Terra Nova on his next attempt to conquer the Antarctic in 1910. Surviving a violent hurricane near New Zealand they made it to Antarctica in January 1911, racing to make the pole ahead of Amundsen and his Norwegian team aboard the Fram.

With his previous experience, Crean was employed as an expert sledger and pony handler proving to be highly capable.

He heroically managed to jump across breaking ice and scale an icewall when his tent was floating away in the night. He managed to raise the alarm and save his two colleagues Garrard and Bowers.

Crean joined Scott on the three legs of their ill-fated treck towards the South Pole. With 150 miles to go Scott decided to send three of the men back. To Crean's great disappointment he was one of the three, despite his great strength, knowledge and experience.

He was not to know then that the polar party would never been seen alive again and endured his own great struggle to bring Lashly and Evans to safety. By February 1912 Evans had scurvy and snow blindness and had to be pulled on the sled. By 18th February it was clear that Evans might soon die, with 35 miles still to go and no more than two days rations, Crean decided he would head for Hut Point alone to get help.

Amazingly he set out without a sleeping bag and only a chocolate bar and three biscuits to sustain him on a 18 hour walk through the harshest conditions on Earth. Totally exhausted, he managed the journey of over 30 miles just escaping a terrible blizzard that would undoubtedly have finished him off. Crean's bravery led to Lashly and Evans being rescued by a dog team and he was later awarded the Albert Medal and Polar Medal by King George and promoted to chief petty officer.

With the failure of Scott's party to return, Crean and his colleagues waited out the harsh winter before 11 of them set out in November 1912 to search for the bodies. Crean noticed an unusual protrusion through the snow which turned out to be the tent inside which lay the frozen bodies of Scott, Wilson and Bowers. The team buried their comrades under a cairn of snow, placing a cross over it, before returning with personal effects, journals and letters which were brought back to England in 1913.

Despite several brushes with death and the tragic loss of his friend Scott, he was not deterred from further exploration. Ernest Shackleton well knew what an asset Crean would be after having worked with him on the Discovery expedition and his heroic exploits on Scott's failed polar attempt. Shackleton selected Crean as his second officer in 1914 and was one of six men for the attempt to cross the entire Antarctic via the South Pole.

In January 1915 their ship, "Endurance", became surrounded by pack ice in the Weddel Sea off of West Antarctica. Crean had another close encounter with death during their attempts to free the ship when he was almost crushed by a sudden movement of ice. The months dragged on as they failed to break free and in November the ship was so damaged that it began to sink.

Recovering what they could the expedition decided to set up Camp Patience on the pack ice with their supplies and three lifeboats. Abandoning Shackleton's plan to cross the ice to Robertson Island, as the ice broke up in the advancing Antarctic summer, they waited hoping the drifting ice would carry them to Paulet Island where there were emergency supplies. This plan failed and as the ice continued to fracture Crean took charge of one of the three vessels on their 7 day treacherous voyage to Elephant Island on the north-west tip of Antarctica.

Many of the men were ill with diarrhoea and sea-sickness but Crean was one of four men still strong enough to find and set up a safe camp for the bedraggled party. Shackleton realized that help was unlikely to come and decided to modify one of the lifeboats for a hazardous voyage to South Georgia, 800 miles away. Initially he had planned to leave Crean at the camp but included him in his 6 man crew after Crean asked to come with him.

On Easter Monday 1916, they departed on the largest lifeboat and endured a horrific two week voyage, reaching South Georgia just as hurricane threatened to dash them against the rocks of the island. Amazingly the little boat survived two days in the hurricane before finally making land minus its rudder on May 10th. Unfortunately the men had landed on the wrong side of the island and had no choice other than to march across the hazardous terrain to the Stromness whaling station.

Crean, Shackleton and Worsley were the only three strong enough to make the crossing. Having already endured unbelievable hardship the three managed the 37 hour march, which they did tied together with ropes, across glaciers and ravines in freezing weather. The other three men were soon rescued and attempts began to save their colleagues on Elephant Island.

Crean, Shackleton and Worsley returned on three different ships in four attempts before they were finally able to reach the 22 men trapped on Elephant Island. Amazingly, all of the men had survived the 3 month wait while their comrades desperately tried again and again to save them.

Crean continued to serve in the navy during World War I after their return, but he returned to Ireland briefly in 1917 to marry his childhood sweetheart Nell Herlihy in Anascaul. Early in 1920 Shackleton asked Crean to join him once again on his ill-fated Quest expedition, which due to a growing family he fortunately turned down. Following a bad fall on his ship Hecia, he was given early retirement in March 1920, returning to Anascaul in the midst of the War of Independence.

Barely a month after Crean's return, his brother Cornelius, a sergeant in the RIC was killed by the IRA in Cork. Tom, aware of the tense atmosphere in Kerry, kept quiet about his service in the Royal Navy and his three Antarctic expeditions although he did call his pub The South Pole Inn, which he opened in 1927.

Tom shunned the limelight, never spoke or wrote about his amazing exploits and refused all requests for interviews, even leaving the pub when people came looking to speak to him about his past. In 1938 he was taken to Tralee hospital with appendicitis but had to be transferred to Cork as no surgeon was available. The delay caused his appendix to burst and Tom died from the resulting infection on July 27th. He is buried in Ballynacourty cemetery in the tomb he constructed himself.

The South Pole Inn changed hands, first to Mike Cahill and then to Den Lenihan in 1953 and then again to the current owner, Tom Kennedy, in 1991. The pub has been leased to the Percival family who renovated the pub, involving the Tom Crean Society to create a permanent record and recognition of his life. The upstairs was converted into a museum of memorabilia and the downstairs features dozens of photographs of Tom and his endeavours.

The Cloosmore Brooch

Just a little south west of Dingle town lies Cloosmore townland (*An Chluais Mhór*) and buried on the beach was one of the most interesting Irish archaeological finds in recent years. The curator at the museum in Ballyferriter (*Baile an Fheirtéaraigh*), Isabel Bennett, was instrumental in reporting the find to the National Museum of Ireland together with Ian Andrew, who discovered the brooch by chance, while walking on the beach at Cloosmore.

Mr Ian Andrew was on a holiday visit to the Dingle Peninsula, where he has family connections. While walking along the rocky shoreline, he noticed a bright light shining between some rocks. After taking a closer look, he retrieved the tiny but exquisite gold ring brooch and subsequently reported it.

The National Museum of Ireland has taken possession of the medieval gold ring brooch (which is barely 2cm in length) since it was found, having acquired it in 2016. In 2018 the brooch was sent on short-term loan of 2 days to *Músaem Chorca Dhuibhne*, in Ballyferriter, only miles from where it was found, during which the author was able to view it first-hand.

Brooches such as this would have been worn by both men and women to fasten their cloaks and ring brooches were often given as love tokens or as betrothal gifts during the medieval period. Approximately 150 such brooches are known in Ireland, but only a very small number are made from gold, which makes this particular find very special.

The Cloosmore brooch is an example of a rare type of 13th/14th century ring brooch with projecting hands. The brooch has a blue stone setting now identified as tourmaline, which is considered to be quite similar to sapphire. There is an inscription in Gothic style lettering on the front of the brooch. While most of the letters are legible, their meaning is unclear and they may represent a type of code. The brooch may possibly have had a magical or talismanic association for the wearer. A number of similar pieces are known from Britain, including an almost identical one from Kent, in south-east England.

Although the brooch is now back in the National Museum of Ireland (in Dublin) it can still be seen in Dingle, as a replica available in either gold or silver, from a local jewellery shop. Local jeweller Jerry Bácaéir revealed to the author that he had the good fortune to receive special permission to photograph and measure the brooch, when it was it was brought to *Músaem Chorca Dhuibhne*. He noticed that the brooch had no signs of wear from the sea, so he concluded that it must have been buried or lost above the tide line, which was extremely fortunate. Mr. Bácaéir was able to produce an exact replica, from which copies are now available in pendant form, on sale in Dingle town.

Marie Antoinette and Rice House

Marie Antoinette is one of the most well-known queens in world history but her connection with the town of Dingle, in West Kerry, is a piece of Irish history that is hardly known outside of Kerry. A plaque erected on the wall of Rice House in 2010, by Dingle Historical Society was unveiled by the Austrian Ambassador to Ireland. Apart from this small commemoration there is little to acknowledge the rescue attempt, that could have saved the French queen's life, which was just one of several failed plans to rescue her.

The plan to save her was organised by James Louis Rice, the son of 'Black' Tom Rice, who was a successful wine merchant from Ballymacdoyle, close to Dingle town. Tom had built up extensive connections with traders and vineyards throughout both Spain and France. James, born in 1730 into a Catholic family, was educated at the Irish Pastoral College in Louvain, Belgium as there were few educational opportunities in Ireland due to penal laws against Catholics. James did well in Belgium and even began studying for the priesthood at the Franciscan seminary in Louvain. However, he abandoned his studies and went on to join the Irish brigade of the Austrian (Hapsburg) army, becoming a cavalry officer and eventually was made a Count of the Holy Roman Empre by the Austrian Emperor, Joseph II, who he had met and befriended at military academy.

Rice even gained a seat on the Emperor's privy council and was one of the trusted soldiers honoured with escorting Joseph's younger sister Marie Antoinette from Vienna to Versailles (near

Paris) in May 1770 to join her new husband, Louis XVI of France. James remained in Paris mostly, in service of the royal family but retained his contacts with his friend Emperor Joseph into the 1780s while the situation in France detiorated in the run-up to the revolution in 1789.

After the death of Joseph II his younger brother Leopold became Emperor of Austria and it was his support for the French Monarchy and his sister that led to France declaring war on Austria in 1792. Louis XVI was separated from Marie Antoinette and their two remaining children, who were themselves imprisoned in the tower of the Temple in Marais. At the behest of Leopold, James Rice began planning an audacious escape attempt to rescue his sister Marie Antoinette, or Maria Antonia as her brother would have called her.

The plan was to bribe the guards at the temple and take her and any other members of the royal family by carriage and a relay of horses to Nantes where a merchant ship, owned by the Rice family business, woud take them to Dingle. The Rice family went so far as to furnish rooms in their Dingle home in readiness for the Bourbon monarchy, although the plan was to eventually send them to London and then on to safety in Vienna, with her brother Leopold, the Austrian Emperor.

Rice enlisted the help of Thomas Trant, a man from Ventry (near Dingle) serving with the Irish Brigade in France, William Hickie from Ballylongford in north Kerry and Count Waters of Paris, who was married to his sister, Mary Rice. Although the plan went off well initially, Marie Antoinette (who was held separately from her husband the King and her two surviving children) refused to leave her family and so the escape had to be abandoned.

After the aboliton of the Monarchy Louis XVI was tried and found guilty of treason and executed at the guillotine in January 1793. After her transfer to the Conciergerie, a final rescue attempt (the Carnation Plot) also failed and the former Queen, in failing health, was executed in October of that same year.

James Rice was able to escape from France and moved to London after which he served in the allied forces (consisting primarily of Britain, Austria, Russia and Spain) in the first of the French Revolutionary Wars. This conflict was known as the War Of The First Coalition, which ended in 1797 with the humiliation of Austria by the French.

In the late 1790s Rice returned to his native Ireland and settled in Limerick, during which he witnessed the United Irishmen's rising of 1798 and the emergence of Daniel O'Connell as a political force. He died at the age of 63 in 1793, as Napoleon continued his rise to power and eventual victory in the War of The Second Coalition. Count James Louis Rice's death was widely reported, both in Ireland and all across Europe, having become quite a hero among monarchists during those turbulent times.

Rice House, which was built in the 1750s, came into the possession of the Church (becoming known as the Old Presbytery) and the house was refurbished during the 19th century before eventually coming into the hands of *Udarás na Gaeltachta*. A plan to redevelop the house and sell it was opposed due to what would have been the effective gutting of the interior and additions and modernization of the exterior. Most of the original features of the house, including the rooms prepared for Marie Antoinette were still in excellent condition, leading to a campaign to keep the historical building in its near pristine state.

Largely due to the work of the Rice House Alliance, planning permission was revoked and the house became a listed building in 2004. Although it was then sold to a local businessman from Dingle, Rice House is now home to Kerry Education and Training Board and albeit partially modernized, thankfully still retains its unique features and period character. The author first visited Rice House in 2016, at the time of writing (2021) it currently hosts KETB and the Citizens' Information Centre.

The Magic Hare

The hare was considered a magical animal in ancient Ireland and the Dingle Peninsula was no exception in this respect. This is one of many such stories that relate to hares, often including strange transformations or witches.

*

There were two men coursing one day, long ago and they had two hounds. They were coming near a house and a hare jumped out of a bush and the two hounds ran after it. The hare jumped in across the door of a house, but not before one of the hounds had bitten off its tail.

The men followed the hare into the house but there was no hare to be found, only an old woman sitting in a chair, unable to get up as she was clearly in some discomfort. The men soon went away with their hounds and continued their hunt for the hare elsewhere, but one of them told his daughter that evening of the strange events and the elderly woman.

The very next day, the hunter's daughter went to the old woman's hovel and she asked the woman her name, but she would not tell it to her. The girl asked the old woman had she any friends in Dingle and she replied that she had a friend by the name of Neligan and so the girl promised to arrange for her to be brought in to see her (as she was seemingly lame) and so she sent word to her father to come fetch them both.

The girl's Father went the following day for her, with his

horse and trap and the daughter was as grey as a ghost, left all alone in the house, as the old woman was gone. She was only fifteen years old but looked a sight for sore eyes, and she never told anything of what happened. She was clearly in shock, and for some time she was not right at all.

Stranger still, a hare had been seen running down the road at Miltown, on the way into Dingle town. The old lady was seen in Dingle not three hours after the girl's father had left to fetch her and people said it must have been the fairies that took her to Dingle in three hours, but of course, we know that she ran there on all fours!

Based on a story collected by P. Ó Gróbhthín from Diarmuid Ó Gróbhthín (*An Cam*/Camp)

The Siege of Smerwick and the Fall of the Geraldines

The Fitzgeralds or Geraldines (Earls of Desmond) and Butlers (Earls of Ormonde) were the two most powerful families in Ireland since the Norman invasion and maintained an intense rivalry down the centuries. This bitter rivalry was effectively ended by the second Desmond rebellion and the subsequent demise of the Geraldine dynasty.

Following the first Desmond rebellion, which had been led by James Fitzmaurice Fitzgerald (who was cousin to Gerald, the 15th Earl of Desmond) Fitzmaurice was pardoned but was stripped of his lands as punishment. His cousin, the Earl, also evicted him from rented land leaving him effectively in poverty. In 1575 James Fitzmaurice fled to France and began seeking the assistance of Catholic powers in Europe, eventually making his way to Rome to petition Pope Gregory XIII for help.

After securing modest assistance, an abortive invasion in 1578 led to a return to Rome and he tried again, in June 1579 under papal authority. Leaving Spain with a small force of Spanish, Italian and Irish troops, Fitzmaurice made his way via the English Channel and succeeded in capturing two English vessels before arriving at Dingle harbour in mid July. On 18th July the party relocated to Smerwick harbour (Ard Na Caithne) further west on the same peninsula. Here they took advantage of a long disused iron-age fort Dún An Óir (fortress of gold) to establish their garrison, creating new earthworks on the promontory.

With the assistance of papal commissary, Nicholas Saunders, Fitzmaurice declared a holy war on Elizabeth I at Dingle, with much ceremony and calling upon Ireland to rise up against the heretic queen, who had been excommunicated in 1570. Fitzmaurice's force was roughly 100 men although two more Spanish galleys arrived soon after with a further 100 troops, but clearly without raising support his rebellion would be easily crushed.

Irked by the English authorities undermining Desmond power, John of Desmond and his brother James entered the fray on 1st August with the assassination of two English officials in Tralee. Having secured some support from relatives, Fitzmaurice himself was only to play a short role in the war. Having travelled north into the province of Connacht to raise further support, he was killed in a skirmish with the Burkes after his men stole some horses from his cousin Theobald Burke.

However, the rebellion was now well underway and leadership was left to John of Desmond who took over much of south Munster, raising some 2,000 men. In response the English Lord Deputy brought 600 troops to Limerick joining forces with Sir Nicholas Malby (Lord President of Connacht) and his force of over a thousand.

Up until now, the Earl of Desmond (Gerald Fitzgerald) had stayed out of the conflict and even gave up his son as hostage as a guarantee of loyalty on condition his lands were not attacked. After plundering of Geraldine territory and the demand that the Earl hand over his castle the situation changed. Gerald refused to leave Askeaton Castle and was then declared a traitor by the

English, leaving him no choice other than to enter the war on the side of the rebels. In November that year he sacked Youghal, in county Cork, escalating the conflict to all-out war and imploring Irish lords to defend Ireland and its Catholic faith.

Following the rising of the O'Byrnes in Wicklow, in July 1580, the English sent a new army of 6,000 men under the new Lord Deputy, Baron Arthur Grey. After an initial humiliating defeat at Glenmalure, Grey marched his men south west into Munster to support English forces there, unleashing a campaign of terror that would long be remembered.

Pope Gregory, whose hand was stoking the fires of war across Europe, intervened once again in Ireland. Having failed to convince Philip II of Spain (who had his own difficulties with the Dutch and Ottomans) to invade Ireland, the Pope did secure ships for Philip to transport a force of around 700 Spanish, Italian and Basque troops under the command of Sebastiano di San Giuseppe.

The small Papal army arrived in Smerwick Harbour on 10th September 1580, joining the small force at Dún An Óir before heading inland to join forces with the Earl of Desmond, John Desmond and Lord Baltinglass. However, the English had somehow gained knowledge of the invasion and with a force of around 4,000, Lord Grey and the Earl of Ormonde marched to cut them off. Meanwhile a naval blockade by Sir Richard Bingham prevented them leaving by sea to join the Irish rebels elsewhere. Trapped in the Dingle Peninsula, Giuseppe was forced to retreat to Smerwick and make what he could of the defenses at Dún An Óir.

In October Grey took his forces as far as Dingle, waiting on supplies and eight cannons to arrive by sea with Admiral Winter at Smerwick. With the Papal forces trapped by the English on one side, the sea behind them and Mount Brandon on the other, Grey was in no hurry. When the artillery finally arrived on 5th November preparations began for the siege, which started two days later.

Hopelessly outnumbered, remorselessly pounded by three warships in the harbour as well as the artillery pieces on land, the rebels stood little chance in a fort consisting mainly of earthworks. Despite this they held out for three days, although Giuseppe rather cowardly tried to bargain with Grey by releasing three local allies to the English. The three men, including a priest (Fr. Laurence Moore) were horrifically tortured to no avail before being used for target practice as the siege continued.

Finally on 10th November the defenders could take no more and surrendered to Grey's terms which were apparently that they would be spared. However, Grey (in his report to Elizabeth I) maintained that he had demanded an unconditional surrender and "that they should render the fort to me and yield their selves to my will for life or death."

Regardless of what was actually agreed, what happened afterwards is well known. The commander Giuseppe, along with 12 of his men emerged from the fort with their flags rolled up and presented themselves to Grey. Troops were sent into the fort to establish that the defenders had laid down their arms and to secure munitions.

Once the fort was secured the 600 or so troops and a few women with them were put to the sword. It is said that the rebels were taken to what is since known as Field Of The Cutting (*Gort A Ghearrah*) and executed one by one. The severed heads of the slain were apparently buried in the field where a monument now stands today, while their bodies were thrown over the cliffs into the sea below.

After the disaster at Smerwick, the tide turned very much against the Desmonds and their rebellion. The coalition began to fall apart, although the war of attrition dragged on for another two years with Desmond's supporters being killed or falling away with the offer of a pardon. In early 1582 John of Desmond met his death while engaged by English troops at the river Avonmore, with his head being sent to the now infamous Lord Grey.

Grey's brutality was notorious but he had still not been successful in defeating the Geraldines. Possibly because of his cruel methods, Grey was recalled to England and the Fitzgeralds' arch enemy the Earl of Ormonde replaced him as Lord Deputy, continuing on with the war that left much of Munster bereft of people, crops and livestock.

By the winter of 1583 the Earl of Desmond stood alone with only a handful of supporters following him into the Slieve Mish mountains to elude English troops. It was here at Glenagenty that Gerald met his end. Desperate and hungry Gerald and his men had stolen a few cattle from the Moriarty clan and supposedly mistreated the sister of the clan chief. Owen Moriarty and his clansmen caught up with the Earl at a small cabin where he was killed and beheaded.

In return Moriarty received 1000 pounds of silver, a vast fortune and Gerald's head was sent to Elizabeth in London, while his body was strung from the walls of Cork city for all to see. His title and all the Geraldine lands were confiscated by the English crown. Attempts to revive Desmond fortunes and the Earldom soon after were a failure and so the once powerful Geraldine dynasty came to a sad and miserable end.

The site of this battle is open to the public and features a rather grim memorial in bronze of severed heads at the entrance! The ramparts of the original defences are little more than grass covered ditches now but the views from the cliff edge are still as spectacular now as they ever were.

Reverend Rowan and the Castle of Castlegregory

Castlegregory (*Caisleán Ghriaire* which means "Griaire's/ Gregory's Castle") is located on the extreme north side of the Dingle Peninsula, about halfway between the towns of Dingle and Tralee. There are two possible sources of the name – the most popular being that Castlegregory was named after the castle built by Gregory Hoare in the 17th century. An alternative interpretation of the name is that it was named after Pope Gregory I (the Great), who some claim to be of Irish origin, although in fact he was a Roman senator's son.

Gregory Hoare, who was of Hiberno-Norman descent, built the castle on lands granted to him by the 14th Earl of Desmond in the previous century. Hoare became involved in a feud with neighbour William Moore, another Desmond tenant, over a dispute over their boundary. The dispute became so serious that the case came before the Desmond *seneschal* court in Dingle, which found against Hoare and he became so outraged that he became paralysed, possibly from a stroke. With Gregory fairly well incapacitated, Hoare's son, Black Hugh became a more powerful figure, finding the opportunity to marry Moore's daughter Ellen, as a means of ending the feud.

Unfortunately as the bridal party made its way through Castlegregory, Gregory Hoare attempted to block their path and prevent the union. William Moore pushed him aside and Hoare died there and then, presumably from the fall. The wedding went ahead as planned but all was not well. During Lord Deputy

Grey's attack on Smerwick (*Dún an Óir*, the Fort of Gold), Black Hugh Hoare was requested to protect his castle against the Irish. Hoare, a loyal subject of Queen Elizabeth I, did as requested going so far as to hold a banquet for Edmund Spenser, Sir Walter Raleigh and other officers at Castlegregory. Hoare's wife Ellen loyal to the Irish cause, resented this intrusion of their privacy and so emptied all of the wine kegs in protest. Black Hugh was so angered by his wife's actions that he stabbed her to death in a fit of temper. Subsequently, Black Hugh was arrested and taken to Gallarus Castle for trial but he died suddenly, close to where his father had died, before the trial could take place.

Black Hugh's only child was a daughter, who married Walter Hussey of Castlegregory and Dingle. Hussey, who was a supporter of the Knight of Kerry, was granted the castle. However, Hussey was a participant in the rebellion of 1641 and so, during the Cromwellian invasion of Ireland, the castle was attacked and laid seige to by Cromwell's forces under Sadlier and leHunt, in May 1649. After several days Hussey fled to Minard Castle but when Minard was later attacked, Hussey and his men were killed. Meanwhile, the castle at Castlegregory was cannoned, burned and finally dismantled. The stones of the fallen castle were apparently removed during the 1880s and today the only remnant of it is an arched door, which stands beside the Spar shop in the village.

*

Reverend Arthur Blennerhassett Rowan was a Protestant priest, writer, poet, antiquarian and scholar, born in Tralee in 1800.

He was involved in local politics and also a major controversy in 1848 when the Tralee Savings Bank, that he was treasurer of, spectacularly collapsed following the theft of £36,000 by solicitor John Lynch. Rowan visited the village of Castlegregory around 1853 where he saw the two arch-stones of the castle embedded in the wall of a house on College Street.

Rowan purchased the arch-stones and had them brought to the garden of his house in Blennerville until his death in 1861. Thereafter, the arch-stones languished in a yard for many years, until a 1903 campaign from *The Kerry People* led to renewed interest and calls for the stones to return to Castlegregory. Tommy Egan of Castlegregory eventually rescued the stones in the 1940s, keeping them in his garden, but eventually they made it to where they are now – in Tailor's Row, very close to the original site of the castle.

Rowan, who was responsible for removing the last surviving piece of the castle from Castlegregory, wrote about the village in his short novella *The Legend of Castlegregory*, which apparently was a vastly elaborated version of a story relayed to him by a local of the village. It was originally published in *Dublin University Magazine*, in February 1851, but later it appeared in *The Kerry Magazine* (which Rowan had edited and founded in 1854), as episodes of one chapter each. It was republished in 1884 in *The Kerry Weekly Reporter*, long after Rowan's death and is now available in full once again in Martin Lynch's 2019 book *Rev. A. B. Rowan and The Legend of Castle-Gregory*.

The Cailleach of *Corca Dhuibhne*

The figure of the Cailleach looms rather menacingly throughout Irish history; portrayed as an ancient goddess of the land, wisewoman healer, the veiled one or a wizened old hag. She is perhaps most famous in Ireland as An Cailleach Bhéara, the hag of the Beara Peninsula but she is also recorded in many place names around Ireland, such as the megalithic sacred site of Loughcrew or formerly Sliabh Na Caillaigh in county Meath, which has it own legend about the Cailleach leaping from hill to hill and dropping the stones there from her apron. In later times she is often seen as a dark and frightening figure who brings the winter with her, disappearing again with the warmth of spring.

She features in many Irish legends such as The Pursuit of Diarmuid and Grainne, in which Fionn engages the magical help of the hag to bring about Diarmuid's demise, athough she is killed in the process. She also features in the stories of Mad Sweeney and Niall of The Nine Hostages as well as many other lesser-known ones.

The hag of Beara is also associated with *Corca Dhuibhne*, (Dingle Peninsula), where it is said she was born. Her birthplace is given as *An Teach Mór* (the great house), supposedly the most westerly house in all of Ireland, at the end of the Dingle Peninsula promontory. She is also given as the ancestor of clan *Chorca Dhuibhne*, after which the peninsula itself is named. The following story is from Dunquin (*Dún Chaoin*), to the west of Dingle.

*

The Cailleach lived on the top of a mountain where the wind blew constantly, she was very hard to approach and no one did. Here on top of the mountain she kept her great treasure. One day, down in the village at the bottom of the mountain, by the sea, the Cailleach rescued a live lobster from a lobster pot left at the front of a house and took it away home with her.

When she got back to her hovel she stowed the lobster in her treasure box under her bed. Another day, when the Cailleach was out, a brave or maybe reckless man climbed up the mountain side, leaning into the ferocious wind, intending to steal the Cailleach's treasure. He entered the tiny house, looked all around and finally under the bed where he saw her old box.

There was a hole in the side of the box, just big enough to fit a hand through and so he reached his hand inside looking for treasure, when the lobster inside quickly clamped onto his hand as he felt around and it would not let go, no matter how much he struggled. So, the man continued to lie on the floor, with his hand stuck in the treasure box, all day long, until he saw the sun beginning to set and the room gradually darkening. At this stage the Cailleach returned. When the old woman saw the man lying there trapped she said, "You have done well, lobster," and with that she took up her hatchet for chopping firewood and chopped off the terrified man's head with a single blow!

Poverty and His Three Wishes

This is a story about an old blacksmith that was back to the west of Dingle (back west) in a very backward place called Coumeen Ole! He was that poor in the world that he went by the name of 'Poverty' and with no one to accompany him, but a little fox terrier that he had by the name of 'Misery', he was that badly off and so poor.

Well one fine summer's day he was outside in the yard sunning himself, when two badly clad men and a lame donkey walked down towards him on the old road that was leading to the main road.

They asked him, if he please could he put a new shoe on the donkey, as the old donkey was lame, for the want of a shoe. He said yes of course and welcomed them, he was so obliging and generous, poor as he was. He went into the forge and searched the forge upside down and he could not find the makings of a donkey shoe of iron and that was little enough, God help him.

Well he came out and begged their pardon and said he was sorry that he couldn't get as much iron as would be needed to make the donkey's shoe. The two men turned back the donkey and went off over the old road. Well, they were halfway over the old road, when he thought of another plan and called them back and got an old shoeing hammer and reddened it and drew out a donkey's shoe out of the old shoeing hammer and drove it under the donkey. When the donkey was shod they asked him what was the charge.

"Is it for me to charge poor distressed craters like ye for a donkey shoe? I'd rather cut my throat first." So they thanked him and said that as he was so generous they'd give him any three wishes he'd ask for.

He said alright and one of the men said to him what was the first wish he'd ask for and the 2nd man shoved over to him & shook him and told him to wish for Paradise. Poverty told him to mind his own business and that he'd wish for anything he'd like. So the first wish he asked for was - that of the one and only old súgán chair in the house, whoever should sit in it that he or she couldn't get up off the chair until himself would release them.

Poverty had a big apple tree growing opposite outside the door and it used to be drooping with apples in the harvest time and it was the principal means of his support and the young lads of the place used to be robbing them when it was in full fruit. The second wish he wanted was that whoever would go up in the apple tree that he or she couldn't come down until himself would release them.

Well the second man was all through with pushing into him and telling him to wish for Paradise and the old blacksmith had all the time been telling him to mind his own business. Well alright! He was told that it was granted. Finally, the third wish was that whatever he'd put into the pocket of his trousers that it couldn't leave until he himself would take it out. Well all three of the wishes were granted to Poverty and the two raggedy men thanked him for his help and walked away with their donkey.

Some two weeks after, a well-clad gentleman walked over to him and had great sympathy and told him that he was very badly off here. Well he said, "If you promise to come with me in ten years time, you'll have everything you want, money and food and drink up till then." So he promised him that he would go with him in ten years time.

That very day, ten years later, the gentleman walked up to him again and asked him was he ready now and asked him was he up to his promise? The blacksmith told him that he would go with him, but he told him "sit down in that chair" until he'd washed himself and got ready. When he was ready, he came out of the room and told him "come on now." So the gentleman made an attempt to get up off the chair and he could not. He made several attempts but failed. The gentleman couldn't rise off the chair so he called out and roared. The blacksmith Poverty asked him would he give him ten years more, in order to release him. He said he would of course, so the blacksmith released him.

The gentleman went away and that very day, ten years later, he came again and two more men with him. He asked him was he ready now and he told him he was of course ready. He saw them admiring his tree that was drooping with apples and Poverty told them that they could go out and eat their fill of them, fill their pockets with them too and that the apples would be carried off by the lads of the countryside anyway, once the three of them had left.

So the three of them went up into the tree and commenced picking apples while himself was getting ready, and when he was ready, Poverty came to the door and said "come on in now,

I am ready now." When they made an attempt to come down from the tree, they couldn't stir. And so he asked them, if he released them, would they give him ten years more and they of course agreed to this.

They went away as promised, and that very day ten years later, the old gentleman came again, but this time with seventy-seven men with him. They spoke to him very roughly and viciously and gave him all manner of abuse.

They told him he should be up to his promise and Poverty said he would be. They commenced to abuse him further and he asked them to calm down and rest a while, but they were the gentleman plus seventy-seven against just himself, so they paid him no heed. They said that they could get into a snuff-box and get out again if that was required to get him to come. So, Poverty bet them that they could not do it and he pulled his snuff box out and left it down on the table for them to jump into. To his astonishment, by some form of magic, the 78 men shrank down and leapt into the tiny box! As soon as he had them inside the snuff-box he clapped on the cover and put it into his pocket and left it there.

The men commenced to roar and scream to be let out but they were smothering in his pocket and they were all crying for mercy. He asked them would they give him another ten years if he released them, which of course they agreed to. And so, once more he released the gentlemen and his huge entourage, who duly left as promised. Before half the ten years were up the old blacksmith, nick-named Poverty, died one morning and his faithful old fox terrier died that evening.

When he went to the gates of Heaven St. Peter opened the door and when he saw who was there he told him he was not wanted here. St Peter told him that when he was told to ask for Paradise, that he did not and that he could not enter the gate or any other into Heaven.

Poverty went wandering and eventually came to another entrance of Paradise and when the man at the gate opened the gate to him, he almost banged the gate into his face. The gatekeeper told old Poverty to go about his business, and that Heaven had seen enough of him before. Poverty had no choice but to return to Earth and wander for all eternity in spirit form, until the end of days. And so, he became called *Domhnall na Gréine* (Donal of the sun) going about the country ever since.

Based on a story collected by S. Ó Murchadha from Nioclás Ó Finn (*An Cam/* Camp)

Fungie, the Dingle Dolphin

Fungie had become a much loved attraction around Dingle town, being a permanent resident of Dingle Harbour, believed by many locals to spend his quiet time in a cave near the entrance in Dingle Bay. Sometimes also referred to as 'The Dingle Dolphin', he was first spotted in 1983 by the local lighthouse keeper Paddy Ferriter, although now the lighthouse is fully automated and no-one lives there anymore.

It is thought by some that Fungie was named after the lighthouse keepers' nickname (supposedly Fungi), as he was the first person to have seen the dolphin, although another source says the name comes from a Dingle fishermen who was teased by his friends for taking an interest in the dolphin, at a time (early 1980s) when it was not typical to do so. He was also being teased for trying to grow a beard, which resulted in the nickname Fungus. Hence the dolphin became known to locals as "Fungus's dolphin" and within a brief period of time the name got abbreviated to just Fungie and it stuck.

Since his first appearance, in 1983, Fungie remained in or around Dingle Bay, residing there into his old age at the time of his disappearance in October 2020. Shortly after his arrival, the corpse of an adult female dolphin was found in the bay, possibly at Milltown beach, whether this was Fungie's mother or partner is unclear. Wild dolphins rarely live past their 20s, but Fungie was estimated to be at least 40 years of age, possibly as old as 55 and the Guinness World Records recognised him as the world's oldest known solitary wild dolphin.

The author was fortunate to meet Martin Knightly (in 2021), the first person to swim with Fungie. "The day after Fungie was first seen I went swimming at *Binn Bán* (Beenbawn) this was in the summer of 1983. I was swimming away, not paying much attention to anything when I saw Nuala Moore (the famous endurance swimmer) waving at me from some distance away. I was rather confused until I saw this long shadow in the water right by me, which must have been 8 feet long. It was Fungie, come over to see me and he swam along side me for a good while – I was the first person in Dingle to swim with Fungie, but certainly not the last."

When asked about how Fungie arrived, Martin had this to say: "Possibly his partner died, they mate for life, and Fungie just stayed around. He certainly was not a pup so I doubt the other dolphin was his mother."

Fungie was famous for his playful interactions with surfers, swimmers, kayakers and divers and with the tourist boats. In general it is rare for dolphins to seek out human contact and Fungie is the only recorded occurrence of a dolphin interacting in such a way with humans in the wild in Ireland. Later in his life Fungie was injured by a boat propeller, the scars from which were clearly visible on the top of his body, the author saw Fungie up close on several occasions and can confirm the unsightly scars behind his head. Fortunately, Fungie was not seriously injured and continued to interact happily with both boats and swimmers until he disappeared, after 13th October 2020.

People still visit Fungie today, in the form of a life-size effigy of him, next to the departure point for the former Fungie boat tours. The bronze sculpture was created by American sculptor and environmentalist James 'Bud' Bottoms (1928 - 2018) for Dingle's Millennium project. Mr Bottoms who wrote children's books on ethics and campaigned for the environment was from Santa Barbara, California, USA, which is a sister city of Dingle. The bronze life-size statue of Fungie was unveiled in a special millennium ceremony at Dingle Marina, next to the Tourism Office on 2nd January 2000.

Previous to his final disappearance, Fungie had never disappeared for more than 24 hours, as confirmed by local fishermen and boat tour operators. It was reported that Fungie was spotted 6 months later, off the coast of Kinsale, but this is highly unlikely. Marine experts state that it is most likely that he died of old age or left the bay with a pod of dolphins that was spotted in the Dingle area around the time of his last know sighting.

There were even rumours that Fungie had been shot and killed. Local boat tour operator Jimmy Flannery dismissed these claims as sensational nonsense: "I did the trips for 33 years. I just couldn't imagine that anyone would have harmed him. I've heard the stories, rumours from different individuals but again my honest opinion on that one is that it is gossip."

Several boats have conducted hunts for Fungie, with local search parties scouring the waters around Kerry. Jimmy Flannery stated to a national newspaper that Mallow Search and Rescue had also been called in to conduct underwater searches in case Fungie's body was lying on the bed of the bay, either dying from old age or a more malevolent cause. "The reason that I got

Mallow Search and Rescue to come up and dive where Fungie was, was to put those rumours to rest."

What happened to Fungie remains a mystery, but after 37 years in Dingle Harbour, he will be missed by locals and tourists alike. Fungie's legacy can hardly be overstated - before he arrived Dingle was just an ordinary Irish fishing village, that had relatively few tourists, most of whom came because of the filming of "Ryan's Daughter" in the area. In the decades since his arrival, Dingle has grown in size, in part to accommodate the flood of tourists, attracted by his joyful aquatic antics and the number of annual visitors in recent years is now running to over a million per year.

Many people, including the author, like to imagine that Fungie just quietly left for new waters, perhaps to end his days with his own kind in the wild, as nature intended.

The Villain of Castlemaine

There was a man in Castlemaine living in a house very near the edge of the village, by the river Maine and he was called Sommers. There used to be jobbers lodging with him and unknown to any of them, he had a trap bed. When a man would get into the trap bed it would open and he would fall down through a sluice, into the Maine and get drowned.

He used to have all their money and possessions left behind and thereby made a good living for himself. One day there was a man come to Castlemaine for the fair and he lodged with Sommers the night before the fair took place. He had a dog with him and just as he was going into bed the dog caught hold of him by the tail of his shirt. He kicked the dog and made a second attempt to go into the bed but the dog caught him again. He kicked the dog again a second time in disbelief.

The man was making a third attempt to get into his bed when the dog jumped on himself and as the trap opened the dog fell down through the bed and disappeared. The man examined the bed and saw that there were springs and secret levers and that when you leaned on the spring it would give way, with the bed swinging down so that you would fall down and drop down into the river, after which the bed would close up again.

The man put on his clothes and waited till everyone had got up in the morning. Out in the kitchen he went very quickly and found his dog sitting outside the front door of the house, waiting for his master. He went to the RIC (police) and reported the matter to them. The constables came right away and inspected the whole thing. Wiley old Sommers tried to run off but he was arrested, tried and transported for life to Van Diemen's Land, but none of the previous murders could be proven. From that day to this, the hole where the men were drowned by is called Poll Sommers' Hole.

Based on a story collected by Eoghan Ó Domhnaill from Séamus Ó Domhnaill (An Cam/Camp)

Minard Castle

Overlooking the sea, Minard castle is a short drive from Lispole village, only a few miles east of Dingle town. It stands on a plain that slopes sharply down to The Bay of Stone, (*Béal na gCloc*) Kilmurry beach (*Trá Cill Mhuire*). Today the castle is on private land belonging to a local resident and it is not open to the general public, in part because of the risk of falling masonry.

It is one of three remaining castles built on the Dingle Peninsula by the Fitzgerald branch of the family, known as the Knights of Kerry, the other two being Gallarus Castle and Rathinane Castle, both of which are west of Dingle town.

The castle is a rectangular tower house constructed from roughly dressed sandstone blocks with strong mortar, which once stood 4 stories high, although today there are only three, with no floors intact you can see only the vaulted remains of the two lower floors, rafter holes and the fireplaces that once kept the castle warm, which the author was lucky enough to see in person a few years ago. It was built in the 16th century by the rebellious Fitzgeralds, but ended up in the hands of Walter Hussey, who married into the Fitzgeralds in the 1600s. In 1650 Cromwell's forces attacked Hussey at Castlegregory Castle (on the north side of the peninsula), which was completely destroyed. However, Hussey escaped with his men before it was demolished and fled via the mountain pass *Macha na Bó* arriving on the south side of the peninsula, by Annascaul Lake and finally pressing on to Minard castle to make his last stand in what was a much stronger castle. Even so, the castle

could not withstand the constant barrage of cannon fire of the Cromwellian army, who encamped at *Cathair na nAcraí* when they caught up with Hussey. Following the bombardment, the English detonated charges at each of the castle's corners. The castle was badly damaged with one wall, (facing the sea) completely collapsing, but despite the best attempts of the attackers, the castle still stood. Hussey and all the occupants of the castle fled out but were subsequently killed by the forces of Le Hunt and Sadler, in a desperate battle outside the ruins, that spared none of the Irish.

A historian of the time commented that the ruined castle was "a defiant and embattled symbol of the dauntless spirit of resistance to foreign domination that first called it into existence." A testament to the skill of the builders, some 370 years after it was ruined, the 3 remaining walls are still intact, but home only to a few nesting birds.

The following poem by Annascaul poet Tom O'Donnell (1904-1973), who is buried in Ballinclare, commemorates the destruction of the castle and the brave defence by the occupants.

There's a castle below by the waters
Where the wild waves croon all the long day,
And their song is of sorrow and laughter
As they kiss the brown rocks of the Bay.
And my thoughts fly away o'er the long years,
O'er the years to a far yesterday,
And I picture an old world of glory
Where the walls now are broken and grey.

From the castle the sweet notes are stealing
Of music far over the Bay,
And the harpers are softly beguiling
Dull care and dull sorrow away,
The soldiers within they make merry,
And they drink to the long, long ago,
The toast is The Kingdom of Kerry,
Benburb and The Gallant Owen Roe.

But a black shadow fell on the water
On the summer that Cromwell came o'er,
When the gay sons of music and laughter
Would throb in the breeze never more,
Long they fought 'gainst the might of the Saxon,
Gainst the musket and dread cannonball,
They fell 'neath the flag of their country.
And sleep near the old Castle wall.

And now there is left of its glory
The great walls and an old-world air,
And the old folk will tell you the story
Of the sieges and battles that were,
And they that when wild storms are breaking
And the wind's blowing in from the sea,
You can hear mid the roar of the tempest
The brave voice of a lost chivalry.

Tom O'Donnell

The Famine on the Dingle Peninsula

Corca Dhuibhne was one of the most isolated and poorest areas of Ireland during the 19th century, even before the great famine of 1845-1849. In 1841, the peninsula had a population of 35,815, while county Kerry as a whole had a population of 293,880.

Subdivision of land into small-holdings had been occurring in rural Ireland since the reign of William III onwards, in most cases tenant farmers paying rent to landlords or to tenants who sublet their land in smaller parcels. Every family sought to rent land if it did not own land and for 90% of the population that was the case – they had to rent the land, or otherwise use 'the long acre', by the side of the road, if they had no other option, although this was not advisable.

The French traveller Gustave de Beaumont observed in 1837 that "the Irish Catholic finds only one profession within his reach and when he has not the capital necessary to become a farmer he digs the ground as a labourer... He who has not a spot of ground to cultivate dies of famine."

Gradually, the cereal and dairy-based diet that had been common for millennia was replaced by potatoes, namely the Lumper variety, which gave a high yield. The high yielding Lumper, that required far less land than say wheat, oats or barley, helped fuel a rise in the Irish population from 6.8 million in 1821 to circa 8.4 million in 1841. Unfortunately, this particular variety of potato was extremely susceptible to blight.

By 1845 one third of all tilled land in Ireland was given over to potato cultivation, which was almost exclusively the Lumper variety. Living conditions for most of the population were extremely difficult at this time, with extortionate rents and very poor quality housing, as well as a very restricted diet.

The onset of a fungus-like organism, the potato blight (Phytophthora infestans) began in 1845, having migrated across Europe, where it caused problems, but generally famine occurred only in isolated pockets where people relied almost exclusively on potatoes, such as one region of Germany.

The potato crop of 1845 on the Dingle Peninsula was infected with blight, but less than half the yield was affected. This caused some concern but not a major panic. However, by the spring of 1846 it was clear that a major disaster was unfolding. With many tenant farmers now unable to produce sufficient food for their own needs, and the cost of supplies rising, disease, starvation and death was a real prospect. In some areas of the peninsula two thirds of the crop was ruined.

Relief Efforts

The government encouraged the creation of 'relief committees', funded by government grants and local donations, to sell food at cost price. By the summer of 1846 there were fourteen of these set up across Kerry, including three on the Dingle Peninsula, while the coastguard was also involved in relief efforts. With a lack of officialdom west of Dingle town, relief efforts in the *Gaeltacht* were disorganized and poorly implemented, to say the least, and the religious divide also proved detrimental.

The arrival of a Board of Works engineer in Dingle, in April 1846, helped to provide employment, as part of the public works of road building etc, but this was of no benefit to those already too ill or malnourished to work. The funds allocated to road building on the peninsula were seven times larger than the previous year and by January 1847 over 5000 people were employed on 9 projects. Of course, during the terrible winter of 1846, the back-breaking road work stopped due to bad weather, which meant that relief effectively ended during that time – further showing the fundamental weakness of the scheme.

Eask Tower, overlooking the town from the other side of Dingle Harbour, was built as a famine relief project - as a 'signal tower' to boats, which was a private project funded by Lord Ventry at the instigation of Rev. Charles Gayer. Hussey's Tower, on the other side of the harbour, was another private famine relief project, funded by a major landlord of the area - Edward Hussey.

Relief provisions were woefully inadequate for the scale of the disaster, and such relief as was available was only for those who were fit to work - those who were unable did not qualify for payment. The relief committees provided cheap food, but for those with no income there was no benefit. The terrible crop failure, coupled with a totally inadequate relief system effectively condemned the already malnourished or ill to almost certain death. It was noted in the *Kerry Evening Post* in August of 1846 – "the scarcity of the year 1846 will be mere child's play to the famine of 1847."

Many of those working on the roads and other relief projects simply dropped dead while they worked. In January 1847, eight people from John Street (in Dingle town) died in one day from dysentery or starvation – the wages and provisions were insufficient to support people and, as a local clergyman wrote, the people were "dying by inches" from exhaustion, disease and malnutrition.

Conditions in Dingle town had rapidly deteriorated due to a huge influx of the poor from the surrounding areas, overloading what relief provisions were available and the temporary workhouses, to breaking point. Local charities provided a 'shell' to convey the dead to be buried in churchyards but huge numbers were buried without a shroud or coffin and many with unmarked graves. The Presentation Sisters, St Vincent de Paul Society and the local clergy were all making efforts to help the starving poor but it was nowhere near sufficient to prevent a catastrophe.

To make matters worse, local shop-keepers were of little help - a local newspaper described them as 'famine mongers' and 'a heartless set' and one town baker was even accused of cheating his customers through a "deficiency of weight" in his loaves.

Soupers

After the Temporary Destitute Act (known as the Soup Kitchen Act) of February 1847, soup kitchens were provided across Ireland for relief of those who could not get access to the workhouses. Prior to this, soup kitchens had been operated on the Dingle Peninsula, by the relief committees and private individuals. These were established at Ballyoughtra, the Great Blasket Island, Dunquin, Monaree, Ballintaggart, Liscarney and Lough. As there were so many to feed some committees decided to distribute uncooked food, which was given to any requesting it. Records for Castlegregory alone show that between June and September 498,222 rations had been issued. Unfortunately those requesting rations included landed farmers, livestock owners, labourers, tradesmen and gainfully employed people. The selfish and greedy were just taking advantage of the free food on offer at the expense of those in genuine need, but these loopholes were eventually closed off, to prevent this immoral behaviour.

The proselytizing of the Protestant clergy, most notably Rev. Charles Gayner (an Englishman employed as chaplin by Lord Ventry), was harshly criticised with the *Kerry Examiner* referring to Gayner and his supporters as 'souper', 'soup-bloated tribe', soup-fattened followers', 'souper perverts' and 'soup-gang' who were already providing some relief before the famine struck but as part of a mission to convert Catholics. Huge hostility, along religious lines, led to him being accused of bribing the Catholic poor with food, to abandon their faith, however Gayner died of typhus in 1848, leading to decline in Protestant conversions.

The Catholic church led a counter offensive against Protestant evangelism, insisting that Catholics refuse the soup at all costs and attempted to provide some relief itself. In truth, the majority of soup provisions (inadequate as it was) were provided by the government, not by Protestant evangelists, with no requirement or pressure to convert, or any other coercion. However, the damage was done – leading many to choose starvation over accepting offers of relief.

The worst year of the famine was undoubtedly 1847, known as 'Black 47', but huge numbers of deaths from starvation continued to be recorded over the winter of 1847-48 and still large numbers in the winter of 1848-49. As well as actual starvation, those weakened by malnutrition were more likely to succumb to diseases such as typhus, dysentery, cholera and consumption (tuberculosis).

Population Decline

Most emigration during the famine in Ireland was voluntary, in that it was not a result of deportation or coercion. Obviously, most of those who left would have preferred to stay with their families, but faced with grinding poverty and the prospect of starvation, many saw leaving the country as the only viable option.

Some assistance was provided to those who wished to leave Ireland. The *Tralee Chronicle* details a total of 674 people who left Dingle via assisted emigration including one group of 116 who left on the Hurron from Blennerville on June 19, 1851. A group of twenty girls left Dingle Workhouse for Australia under the Earl Grey scheme.

The population of the Dingle Peninsula fell by 23.7% between 1841 and 1851, which was far higher than the national figure of 18.9%. The greatest drops in population in the Dingle Peninsula were in Ballyferriter (-49.9%), Dunquin and the Blasket Islands (-48.2%) and Minard (-48.4%) followed by Kilquane (-43.3%), Kilmalkedar (-43%), Garfinny (-44%), Kinard (-43%) and Ventry (-42%). This tragically accelerated still further following the famine, with 30.4% of the remaining population of the peninsula choosing to emigrate between 1851 and 1891.

Dingle and its environs were effectively hollowed out by the famine deaths and by those leaving to escape the famine, plus mass emigration in subsequent decades.

This trend of emigration decreased but did not come to an end until the 'Celtic Tiger' years in the early 1990s, when the Irish and the diaspora began returning home. Today descendants of the families of the Dingle Peninsula are scattered all over the world, in part fueling the massive wave of tourism. Many of those visiting Dingle come not just to visit this beautiful place, but to see and connect with the land and people of their ancestors.

The Hare Stone

Hares are often regarded as magical creatures in Irish folklore, in the *Schools Collection* of the 1930s there are hundreds of stories that feature hares, and in county Kerry alone there were well over a hundred hare stories collected by school children. Often hares are linked with magic, witches or ghosts and the Dingle Peninsula has its very own variant linked to an ancient menhir, or standing stone, at Graigue (*An Ghráig*) near Lispole, that is split in half.

The stone is associated with a story of Fionn Mac Cumhaill and his two magical hounds Bran and Sceolan who had both once been human. Seemingly the stone split in half during this episode in which the two hounds failed to catch the magical white hare, but sadly this is a case of a well-known story being adapted and changed to suit local events. The standing stone at Graigue was apparently whole in the early 1800s and split in half some time after the Ordnance Survey visit of that time. Well, as they say often – why let the truth spoil a good story?

*

Fionn Mac Cumhaill while visiting a local chief at the great fort of Rathinnane decided to go hunting with his two hounds Bran and Sceolan. These hounds were fiercely loyal to Fionn and also magical, as there was no mortal creature that they could not catch. One of them (Bran) was described thus in ancient annals: "*A ferocious, white-breasted, sleek-haunched hound; standing as high as mid-chest of a full grown man; fiery, deep black eyes that seemed to swim in sockets of blood. Sceolan was described as Slightly smaller than the black beast, small headed, having eyes of a dragon, the claws of a wolf, the vigour of a lion; and the venom of a serpent.*"

So with his two trusty hounds, Fionn was confident that he would have no trouble running down the famous white hare, however things did not go as he had planned. No matter how hard they tried they could not catch the hare, which ran both Fionn and the hounds ragged, with its sudden twists and turns, yet it could not escape their pursuit. Fionn soon realized that this was no ordinary hare – but how could his two inexhaustable hounds catch an uncatchable hare? It was like an unstoppable force meeting an immovable object – a stalemate that seemingly could not be broken. After hours of watching and following the shenanigans, all over the Dingle Peninsula, he prayed for assistance from the old gods of the *Tuatha Dé Danann*, just as the party approached the hill near Lispole. As they reached the plateau the two dogs finally began to close in on the hare, as it approached the great standing stone on the plain. But, to Fionn's consternation, the Hare jumped straight at the mighty stone and he watched in awe as the stone split clean in two, with a loud cracking sound, and the magical hare vanished into the gap, never to be seen again.

In 2020 a version of the Hare's Rock story was published by Ponc Press - "*Carraig an Ghiorria*", "The Hare's Rock", with an English translation by Camilla Dinkel. Originally printed in Irish and German, it has been reproduced in Irish and English in a beautiful fold-out format with accordion pleats and stunning illustrations by well-known local artist Bob Ó Cathail.

It tells another, older version, of the above story - of a bet made by Fionn Mac Cumhaill while he was staying at Rathinnane Castle (near Ventry), as to whether his two hounds Bran and Sceólan could catch the elusive great white hare of Dunquin.

The Irish (presumably original) version of the story was written down by Dunquin teacher and storyteller Mícheál Ó Dúbhshláine, who used to tell the tale to visitors and local children, until his retirement in 2003. Mícheál Ó Dúbhshláine had learned the story from Séamus Ó Cíobháin, who lived in the townland of *Gleann Loic,* at the bottom of The Clasach. The story was already ancient in his time and it was previously mentioned by Peig Sayers (who died in 1958), who visited Hare's Rock once on her way to Ventry.

The Lament of the Fairies - *Port na bPúcaí*

The story goes that it was an unusually warm spring evening on *An Blascaod Mór* (Great Blasket Island) and the sea was totally calm. Most of the islanders were fast asleep but a few of them still awake, some out fishing in the near darkness. Two fishermen were silently rowing back in their *currach* (coracle) towards the harbour and meanwhile an old woman wrapped in her long shawl was gathering up mussels at low tide, on *Trá Bhán* (White Beach). There was also an old fiddler taking the opportunity to have a nip of whiskey, while his wife was out, after playing one last tune as he sat on the stool outside his home.

It was these few souls that heard the music – a sudden and faint but haunting melody that rose up out of the sea. The gentle breeze carried the song to the islanders and the men in the *currach* stopped rowing and just sat listening to the beautiful lament that miraculously rose from the depths. The old woman folded up the mussels in her skirt, returning back home to call her husband. To her surprise he was already outside the house, sat on a stool with an empty glass and his fiddle on his lap, mesmerized by the music from the sea.

All those who heard the music sat transfixed by its melody, which brought tears to their eyes, quite clearly an otherworldly tune from the spirits of the sea. It is said that they sat there all night, listening to the unearthly music, until the morning sun emerged in the East and the sound slowly faded away.

The old fiddler took up his violin, knowing that he had to

record the melody for posterity, so beautiful was the tune they had heard. He did his best to capture the intense beauty of the ethereal music, but even his skills could not capture it exactly. The tune, as he remembered it, was committed to his memory and from then on transmitted to other local musicians, in what is now known as *Port na bPúcaí* or 'Lament of the Fairies'. In an alternative version of the story, perhaps closer to the truth, fishermen visiting I*nis Mhic Fhaolain* in the Blasket Islands, not far from Great Blasket, heard the tune coming from the mists, with these words:

Is bean ón slua sí mé
Do tháinig thar toinn
Is do goideadh san oíche mé
Tamall thar lear
Is go bhfuilim sa riocht so
Fé gheasa mná sí
Is ní bheidh ar an saol so
Go nglaofaidh an coileach

Is caitheadsa féin
Tabhairt fén lios isteach
Ní taithneamh liom é
Ach caithfead tabhairt fé
Is a bhfuil ar an saol so
Caithfidh imeacht as
Ach beadsa ag caoineadh'n
Fhaid a bheidh uisce sa toinn

Is ná deinig aon ní
Leis an ndream thíos sa leas...

I am a woman from the Fairies
Who has come over the waves
And I was taken at night
For a while abroad
And I am in this state
Under spell of the fairy woman
And I will not be in this world
Until the cock crows
And I must go
Into the fairy fort
It is no pleasure for me
But I must do it
And all that is in this life
Must leave it
But I will be weeping
As long as water remains in the wave
And have no dealings
With the crowd that is down in the fairy fort...

The air *Port na bPúcaí* has been credited variously to Kerry musician Muiris Ó Dálaigh (1910-1990, brother of Tom Ó Dálaigh) and also Seán Ó Riada (1931-1971), but who originally composed it is uncertain. A beautiful new version of it was recorded and released by Dingle *Gaeltacht* singer Muireann Nic Amhlaoibh (with Billy Mag Fhloinn) in 2020.

The Leprechaun and the Old Couple

Long ago a old man and his wife were going to town on a mule and cart they had and as they went towards Derrymore bridge they saw "a little red jacket and green cap" running across the road. The man got out of the car and he ran after the figure and caught hold of him as he was just going into a fort. He asked for a pot of gold and the leprechaun said that he could not give it to him, but that he would give him instead any three wishes he would ask for when they arrived at Tralee. They would get anything they would ask for by saying "I wish I had this", so said the leprechaun.

The man agreed to let go of the leprechaun, who disappeared in an instant, and he went back to the cart, delighted with himself.

The old couple continued on with their journey, and when they got to Tralee, the husband left the woman minding the mule and cart. While the husband was away, a pedlar man came by with sets of old saucepans. "I wish I had some saucepans" were the words that came out of the wife's mouth, and that very minute a set of saucepans left the bundle and fell into her lap.

When the husband came back to her, he asked her if she had wished for anything and so she showed him the saucepans. He got very vexed at this, and in his rage he said "I wish they were stuck to your back, you silly woman!" and so it was, just as he had wished for. He pulled at the saucepans for all he was worth but they were stuck fast to her back, no matter what he did. Presently, the poor woman began to cry at the prospect of forever having the pans stuck to her old back.

Now two wishes were gone and there was nothing for it – the husband had to give the third wish in order to pull the saucepans away from his poor wife's back! Both husband and wife were distraught that the three wishes were gone and wasted and they had only a set of rusty old saucepans to show for their trouble!

Based on a story collected by Pádraig Ó Cinnéide from Tomás Ó Cinnéide (*An Cam*/Camp)

Jack the Thief and *An Gadaí Dubh* (the Black Rogue)

Long ago there was a Colonel who was a very sick man and he had a man working for him as a labourer. The house where the labourer lived was tied on to his own house but it was a very lowly house compared to the colonel's. One day the colonel said that he would get a better job for him, if he was a bit of a thief. The man, who was called Jack, said that he was not a thief by nature, but that he would do his best for the colonel.

The colonel told him to walk twenty miles until he saw a glen in which there was a house with a dim light - this was *Gadaí Dubh*'s house. The colonel said that if the thief asked him his name to tell him, and if he asked him what he was, to say that he was a thief.

So Jack went and he found the house without much bother. He knocked at the door and the *Gadaí Dubh* opened it.

"What is your name?" he asked the man and so he told him.

"What is your way of living?" he said. "I am a thief." said young Jack.

"Very well," said the other, "Sit there and I will keep you the night."

Then Jack sat down as told and stopped there for the night. The *Gadaí Dubh* said that he had another man in the house but that "if you are better than him, I will keep you on."

"All right," said Jack.

The *Gadaí Dubh* had a lot of fat sheep around his land. The next day he sent the first thief with three of the sheep to the fair. He told Jack that if he would steal the sheep from the other man while he was going to the fair, he would keep him on.

And so Jack went before the first thief and he stopped near a wood until he came along. He asked him:

"How much for the sheep?"

"One pound ten each." said the thief.

"Drive them in there to the wood awhile," said Jack, "and I will pay you for them soon."

Then the thief drove them into the wood. They were talking together for a while about who made the best ale, but Jack gave over a bottle of ale but never paid a penny over for them. The first thief was walking around the road never thinking of anything but the chat and the drink.

The next thing, Jack jumped into the wood while the other looked away, as fast as he could and drove the sheep before him home to the *Gadaighe Dubh*. The first thief hadn't noticed his buyer had sneaked off for quite some while, and when he looked for the sheep, they were gone. He searched everywhere for them but he couldn't find them. So he went home to the *Gadaí Dubh* and told him he had lost the sheep.

"You're not much use," said the *Gadaí Dubh*, "But I will give you another chance."

The following day he gave the foolish thief three more sheep. He told young Jack to go and do the same thing as before. And so, Jack went to the wood again, but this time he went into it and sat down inside, out of sight. He stopped there until the stupid thief came with the three sheep. Then he started screeching like a sheep, "Baa! Baa! Baa!"

When the thief heard it he thought the other three sheep were there inside the wood. He did not know the spot exactly where the sound came from, so he jumped into the woods a short distance away from where Jack lay hid, and began looking for them. He left the three other sheep out on the road after him and started searching up and down for the other three sheep.

As quick as a flash, Jack jumped out quietly onto the road and drove the three sheep on the road home to the *Gadaí Dubh* again. The foolish thief searched all the length of the wood for the sheep he had heard, but of course he could not find them. Then finally, after giving up, when he looked for the other sheep on the road they were gone too! Then he had to return downhearted to tell the *Gadaí Dubh* that once again he had lost them. The *Gadaí Dubh* by now had them in his top field after Jack had returned them. Then the *Gadaí Dubh* said that he would keep Jack on instead of the foolish thief. But before he could leave, he asked the silly thief to pay for the six sheep that were lost.

"I have no money." said the foolish man.

"I'll take it out of your wages so." said the *Gadaí Dubh*. So he kept most of the money and then told the foolish thief to go away, with barely any pay for his trouble.

It was coming into the winter and the *Gadaí Dubh* wanted meat to eat. He told Jack that there was a fine bull near the place and that if he could steal him, that it would do them both for the winter. He asked Jack how would they steal him.

"I'll tell you," said Jack. "We'll dress up in grand clothes and pretend to be rich buyers."

"That would not do at all," said the *Gadaighe Dubh*, "because the owner has my picture over the door, so if he sees me he will know it's me."

"What harm?" said Jack, "We'll try it in different clothes."

So they dressed up in grand clothes, with a hat pulled down on the head of *Gadaí Dubh,* and they went to the farmer and pretended to be buying the bull. The bargain was nearly finished when Jack looked at the picture over the door.

"What picture is that?" he said to the farmer.

"That is the picture of an awful thief that is around here," said the farmer, "and they call him the *Gadaí Dubh.*"

"Is there any reward out for him?" said Jack.

"Oh there is indeed," said the farmer "twenty pounds!"

"Give it to me and I will tell you, where he is," said Jack.

So the farmer gave him the twenty pounds.

"Here he is," said Jack pointing right at the *Gadaí Dubh*, who began to run off as fast as his legs could carry him.

The farmer blew his whistle and called his dogs and his servants and sent word to everyone in the village. Very soon, everyone was after the *Gadaí Dubh,* but the cute hoor ducked into the woods and they couldn't catch him. At the same, time Jack stole the bull and drove him home to the house of the *Gadaí Dubh.* When he went into the house, he saw the *Gadaí Dubh* washing his legs in a pot of hot water and picking the thorns from them. While the *Gadaighe Dubh* was running he had had to take off his shoes to go faster, and so his legs were all full of thorns from the hedges and the woods.

"You are a queer man anyway," said the *Gadaí Dubh*.

"Why?" said Jack, "Haven't we the bull and twenty pounds with it?"

So they slaughtered the bull and he did them proud for the winter food.

In his travels, Jack had left his mother in the little house near the colonel's when he was leaving to go to *Gadaí Dubh*, so now he said he should go back and see her. He went to the place, but the little house wasn't there any more. He asked the colonel what had happened it and the colonel said that he had knocked it and built another one for the mother about half a mile away.

"All right," said Jack, "you knocked my house and I'll have yours instead."

The colonel only laughed at this.

Then Jack went to the house built for his mother and found that it was a very small one. To his great dismay, when he went in his mother was very sick and dying. So Jack went to the nearest public house and bought a bottle of whiskey and plenty of eggs. He beat up one of the eggs and put a few drops of the whiskey into it and gave it to his mother to revive her. He gave her the same a few hours after and soon enough she was picking up a bit.

The colonel had sheep grazing in the field where the new house was built. The following day Jack killed one of them and he cooked it for his mother and made soup. When the sheep was finished up Jack went out and brought in a bullock from the field and he did the same with him as with the sheep. Then finally his mother got much better and she lived on.

Then the colonel noticed that a sheep and the bullock were gone. He suspected Jack and told him that he would take no more of his nonsense. The colonel said that if he was such a great thief, he would try him out and see how good he really was. He wagered that if he could steal the sheep from under him in bed that very night then he would give him twenty pounds.

The colonel told Jack that he would have two well-armed soldiers on guard too and he put one of them at each side of the fire, and if they heard him coming they were instructed to shoot him dead on the spot. He told Jack not to try if he had any sense, but if he liked to risk being shot, he could prove his skill as a thief.

"I'll try anyway." said Jack.

The next day, Jack went to the public house and bought two bottles of whiskey. Jack put them inside his coat and walked until he came to a big guttery hole, where he threw himself into it and rolled and rolled about fifteen times in it until he was all covered in mud from his head to his toes. Next he went back to the colonel's house. The colonel had a house in which there were a great many pigs in the sty behind. Jack got a nail to open the sty door and went into the first sty and he laid down with the pigs and began to screech until the men inside the house heard it. The colonel's soldiers came out, and not realizing who he was, carried him in near the fire and gave him a sup of hot milk to pick him up. After a while Jack took out one bottles of whiskey.

"One good turn deserves another." said Jack, and he gave them the bottle.

They put their guns up against the hob and drank the whole bottle between them in no time so that they were sodden drunk. They were beginning to get noisy so Jack gave them the second bottle and soon they began to fight over it. Shortly after they fell over each other in the middle of the floor in a drunken brawl. At this stage, Jack got one of the guns and went upstairs to the colonel's bedroom with it. He put the barrel of it to the old colonel's face and told him to give him the sheep under the bed and the twenty pounds with it too. So the colonel begrudgingly gave him the sheep and the twenty pounds to boot.

"I will get your house too!" said Jack.

"Indeed you won't." said the colonel.

However, a few days later the colonel's wife and mother-in-law died. After the funeral Jack got the colonel's two best horses and went off to the graveyard at night. He dug up the dead wife and mother-in-law, took them out of their coffins and put them both up on the horses. He tied them well with ropes so that they couldn't fall off and put a stout stick in their backs to keep them upright. Then Jack drove them back and into the colonel's yard and the horses began to trot about on the cobbles. The colonel had been asleep but the noise of the horses woke him. He looked out of the window and when he saw his wife and mother-in-law up on the horses in the moonlight he instantly died with the shock of it. When the neighbours saw him the next day they wondered what happened.

"I suppose," they said, "he got some great fright and died on the spot."

After they had a wake and they had buried him, Jack said that he was the nearest to the house and had claim to it.

"He knocked my mother's house," he said, "and I will have his as a replacement, as he was childless."

The villagers all thought this was fair enough, so clever old Jack the thief got the house too in the end and lived in it thereafter with his mother.

Based on a story collected by Séamus Aghas from Donnchadh Ó Séaghdha (*An Cam*/Camp)

The Dingle Sturgeon

The story of the famous sturgeon caught and lost, and caught again in Dingle was brought to a new audience through Red Fox Theatre's highly acclaimed and hilarious play, *Catch of The Day: a Sturgeon Story*. The author was lucky enough to see the final performance of the play at Dingle's Beehive Theatre, which included one of the protagonists in the audience – none other than John Francis Brosnan, who caused a commotion by letting the huge fish back into the water. Interviewed by the author in 2021, John Francis had this to say about the whole episode:

"When I was 19 years old I was a fisherman on the boat 'Reviving Swan'. One day at the harbour this boat arrived in called 'The Morning Star', skippered by Joe Welch, which had caught a huge sturgeon. We had never seen one before or afterwards as these were unknown in Dingle waters, this was back in 1966."

"I just went in to look at this fish, which had been kept alive with wet sacks. It was a big deal, a real event as this was what is described as a royal fish, from which caviar is made (the roe/eggs). It might be sent to the President of Ireland, such a fish, and there were lots of people gathered and excited and someone shouted over at me 'throw him out'."

"What they meant was throw him (actually a her) out onto the pier, but what did I do? I wasn't thinking and in a split second I threw it into the sea! There was fierce excitement as the crew were trying to recatch the fish but to no avail, as I saw it swimming away - it was gone."

Some four hours later there was another sturgeon caught by another John (Sean) Brosnan who owned the 'Ard Ide' boat. The excitement started all over again, but this fisherman had been jailed by the President for being an IRA member, at The Curragh, and he was not inclined to give Dev (Éamon De Valera) the fish. De Valera was not too keen to accept the royal fish from an ex IRA man anyway. and so it was suggested that he give the fish to the Poor Clare nuns, down in Cork, instead.

The "cute hoor" fish buyer, who took the fish off of Brosnan's hands, one Micheál Keane, instead sent a box of regular fish to the nuns, thinking they'd be none the wiser and sent the sturgeon over to Billingsgate fish market in London, England. The nuns had invited local dignitaries for a special meal to enjoy the fish, but of course it turned out not to be what they had expected. Meanwhile, the now famous sturgeon was sold and where do you suppose the fish finished up? It was bought for the kitchens of Buckingham Palace and one can assume it ended up in the stomachs of Queen Elizabeth and the British royal family. That fish was worth a small fortune, perhaps 150 punts at the time, which would be well over €3000 in today's money.

The Charger Shipwreck

Shipwrecks off of the Kerry coast were not uncommon and a particularly unlucky one took place in 1890, as reported by *The Dundee Courier & Argus*, Tuesday, November 18. "News reached Belfast yesterday of the loss of the Barque Charger during the recent gales in the Atlantic. The mate and crew were saved by the steamer City of London. The Charger was bound from Dalhousie for Belfast with deals." The Charger was a barque (*barc*), 3 or 4 rigged vessel, out of Belfast and owned by Thomas S. Dixon, also of Belfast. The following story was collected in the 1930s by Cait O'Connor from an unknown source, but most likely a family member who remembered the incident, although the date given in the story is incorrect.

*

The Charger was the name of the first ship which was wrecked around here. She was wrecked on November 24th 1890. This ship had a loading of deal boards. She was coming against the wind and her sails got tattered and torn. Then the crew left her with, only one black cat aboard and afterwards this cat was kept by a Tralee merchant as a souvenir.

The first man that went to her after she was wrecked was an Ashe man from *Mahrabeg*. It was a bright moonlight night and it was also a very fine winter night, so that the people of the place had no bother in drawing in the boards and making them up in rafters at the seaside. After the wreckage of the ship a lot of people were in a hurry to her, to know which of them would find the Logbook because there was a large sum of money offered for it - and it was this Ashe man that found it. There were police along the strand minding the timbers but this they did not do effectively, because they were stolen in the night. Then the police searched the local gardens but the timber that was left was bought up by the Tralee merchants. It was a great year for the poor people because they earned a lot of money rafting the timber. The lights were left lighting in the Charger because the sailors had not time to quench them.

Shortly after there was another ship wrecked called the 'Port-Yarrock'. She was wrecked on the 6th of July 1893. She is said to have been a hundred days in the sea. This ship was loaded with copper and the crew had intended that after emptying the copper they would go to Queenstown (Cobh) for more orders. Very suddenly the weather got bad so she anchored close to Brandon and the crew went into Brandon.

Here they got a great entertainment and when the sea calmed down they went back to their ship again. The storm rose a second time but now it was twice as bad, so she drew her anchor into Kilcummin Strand and got wrecked there. There were twenty men on board, including Captain Forbs, so when she got broken all the crew sank to the bottom and got drowned. There was a great crowd in the strand when the drowning took place and the drowning voices could be heard calling for help far and wide. However the night was so bad that a canoe could not float in the water and on this account the poor sailors had no chance of being saved. The crew were in Brandon two nights before the sinking and Forbs went to Tralee. He got a call to anchor in another harbour but he refused. Some days after the wreck, the dead bodies were driven in by the wind to Kilcummin Strand and were buried in Kiliney. Some years after there was a fine song made about them. The following is a verse.

God bless the poor parents
That they have left behind,
And far away from Brandon Bay,
In sorrow you will find.
To think upon those sailor boys
Who were lost by Kilcummin's shore.
It is all in vain for to regain
Their sailing days are o'er.

This song is said to be composed by a brother of Frank Neill.

Based on a story collected by Cait Ó Connor (Na Machair/Magharees)

A Ghostly Treasure

The time in which the events narrated in this story occurred is in the 1650s, when a party of English soldiers under the command of the General Edmund Ludlow overran this part of Kerry. In his own letters he admits carrying off five thousand head of cattle, sheep and horses, and killing a great number of people. None escaped him except those who took refuge among the Slieve Mish mountains, which traverse the Dingle Peninsula.

At that time there lived in a part of Milltown Demesne a family named Bushfiels - a branch of a very ancient family. The head of the family at that particular period was a sort of recluse, living with two servants - an old man, and an old woman. Bushfiels was reputed to possess three ferkins full of gold, as at that time there were no banks or other secure places in which to keep money. Hearing that the soldiers were approaching he called his servant, and bade him to take the gold and bury it in a secure place where it would be safe until the soldiers had disappeared.

Bushfiels waited until the servant returned and he inquired if he had hidden the gold according to instructions. The man answered where it was stowed and immediately Bushfiels produced a blunderbuss & shot the servant on the spot, so that no one would be wise as to the hiding place. Bushfiels then escaped to a place of safety, and the old woman also escaped into the surrounding woods, although unknown to Bushfiels she had seen the man servant bury the treasure. Meanwhile, the house was burned to the ground by the soldiers but they found no gold or valuables beforehand.

Years, probably centuries, passed by and although the old servant woman's story still was handed down by tradition, through the ages, no one attempted to seek the hidden treasure. At length three brave men resolved to try for the fortune, which was reputed to be hidden beneath a huge elm tree. They went searching on a bright moonlight night, and dug a trench all around the tree.

Then one of the men struck something which sounded like iron, and immediately the cry of hounds and the sound of a horn sounded very close, and fierce hounds ran through the trench and all around the tree. The men ran for their lives in fear, to the shelter of the wood close by. Coming back after a while they found the trench filled in and the ground around the tree looking as if it had never been disturbed by a spade. The three men went back to their homes, and after a short time each was seized with a fatal illness, and strange to say, the symptoms in each case were the same.

Some years later, a younger generation scoffed at the idea of ghostly riders, horns and hounds. Two young and powerful men, who did not believe that the treasure was guarded by ghosts, went secretly one night, after having surveyed the ground for some time previously, and commenced digging operations.

As before, the spade struck the iron, and immediately, a large and terrible man stood before them, accompanied by the sound of hounds and horns blowing. The look he bestowed on the two strong men froze the blood in their veins and, for all the treasure the earth contained, they would not undergo the same experience again. These two men were in the same manner as their predecessors, seized with a fit of illness which again proved fatal, the symptoms being similar to those in the first cases, many years back. Other efforts also met with disaster, and as the years rolled by, people wisely refrained from interfering or digging around the old elm tree, until eventually the treasure was forgotten.

Based on a story collected by Peggy O'Sullivan from William Hanafin (Castlemaine)

Scotia - from Egypt to Ireland

Long ago, perhaps some time around or after 1334 BC, an Egyptian princess came to live and die in Ireland. Her name was Meritaten and she was the daughter of the powerful pharaoh Akhenaten, who ruled all of Egypt, but she has become known to us simply as Scotia or Scota.

The pharaoh Akhenaten was deeply unpopular due to his worship of the single god the Aten, displacing the many gods and the cult of Amun, and it is often suggested that he was murdered in order to restore the old order. It was through his famous son Tutankhaten (Tutankhamen) that the old gods of Egypt and their priesthood were reinstated. It is thought that Scotia (Meritaten) was the eldest daughter of Akhenaten and his wife Nefertiti. It is known that Scotia fled Egypt after the death of her father, with a huge entourage.

According to Walter Bower's 15th century manuscript *The Scotichronicon*, Scotia was an Egyptian princess and daughter of a pharaoh who fled from Egypt with her husband Gaythelos (*Goídel Glas*), with a large following of people who arrived in a fleet of ships. They settled in Scotland for a while amongst the natives, until they were forced to leave and relocated to Ireland. Here they formed the Scotti, and their kings went on to become the high kings of Ireland. In later centuries, they returned to Scotland, defeating the Picts, eventually giving Scotland its name. Scotia is also sometimes given as the wife of Míl the leader of the Gaels and also wife of Eremon (*Érimón*) in the A*nnals of the Four Masters* and *Lebor Gabála Érenn*.

According to legend Míl led his people, referred to as the Milesians, from Scythia, to conquer the distant land of *Ciar* in south-west Ireland. The Milesians were thought to come from Scythia, and as described in *Lebor Gabála Érenn, The Book of the Taking of Ireland*, they invaded what is now known as the Dingle Peninsula, in county Kerry.

With the assistance of the famous druid Amergin, the Milesians managed to gain a foothold in Ireland and fought against the *Tuatha Dé Danann* in the *Sliabh Mis* mountains, according to *Lebor Gabála Érenn*:

"At the end of three days and three nights thereafter the Sons of Míl broke the battle of Sliab Mis against demons and Fomoraig, that is, against the Túatha Dé Danann. It is there that Fás (sic lege) fell, the wife of Únis son, Uicce, after whom "the grave of Fás" is named, between Sliab Mis and the sea.

Scotia daughter of Pharaoh, king of Egypt, also died in that battle—the wife of Érimón son of Míl. For Míl's son Bile went a-voyaging into Egypt, four ships' companies strong, and he took Scotia to wife, and Érimón took her after him. In that night on which the sons of Míl came into Ireland, was the burst of Loch Luigdech in Iar-Mumu.

'Shah Mis' - that means the worst mountain which they found after coming into Ireland, for there they fought their first battle in Ireland."

How Scotia died exactly is unknown but it is said that she was thrown from her horse over-looking the river that runs through *Gleann Scotín* or Scotia's Glen to this day. Two stone graves are to be found on the southern side of the river, barely 10 metres apart. It is said that these are the graves of Scotia and her horse, but equally it could be Scotia and Fás. Neither grave has been excavated as yet, so we have no way of knowing who is actually buried there.

The author has visited the graves on many occasions, one of which was during heavy rain, and it appeared that there were very faint hieroglyphics on one of the wet stones. Maybe one day the site will be excavated by archaeologists and the truth of the legends will be proven, who knows?

The Ghost of Slieve Mish

Old people in this district still talk of the ghost which haunted the pass of *Gleann Scoheen (Scotín)* or Scotia's Glen which contains the grave of Queen Scotia, in the foothills of the Slieve Mish mountains. There is not a shadow of a doubt that such a spirit haunted this lonely pass.

The spirit would come in various shapes, and not only struck terror into the hearts of the people for miles around, but actually killed some of them. At one time it would appear as a cow, at another time as a horse, sometimes again as a sow surrounded by a litter of bonhams, but always it finally changed into a fierce and terrible woman in the end.

Sometimes people escaped her wrath by being very civil and obliging, but others lost their lives on the spot, or got a severe beating, from the effects of which they later died.

Some few lucky people managed to survive the encounter unscathed: let us take for instance the case of a man named Bryan Connor, a native of Tralee. Being out late on business and in a hurry to get home, he had no option but to ride his horse through this pass (it being a shortcut through the mountain from Castlemaine to Tralee). Seeing a feeble old woman on the road he offered her a ride on his horse. The seemingly weak old woman instantly sprang up on the horses's back, like a youngster, to the great surprise of Bryan.

They had not gone very far when the horse began to tire. The man remarked that he did not know what had come over his horse. Instantly the woman jumped down from behind him and said to him "I had at first intended to kill you, but your kindness has spared your life", and so the man continued his homeward journey in safety.

Two travellers named Ó Shea (a man and his wife), were not so fortunate as Byran Connor. They somehow got in a row with the old woman, entered into a fight with her and both were killed. This spirit haunted the pass for many years, perhaps even centuries, until a parish priest, Father John Carmody of Castlemaine, banished her. A part of the mountain is still known as the "Spirit's Leap", most likely in reference to the strange shape-shifting ghost that resided there.

Based on a story collected by Peggy Kavanagh from William Hanafin (Laharn, Castlemaine)

The Legend of Annascaul Lake

In past times Annascaul Lake (*Loch an Scáil*) was regarded as a magical place, in fact the name Annascaul comes from the Irish (*Abhainn an Scáil*) both names referring to the lady Scál or Scáil (*Scál ní Mhurnáin*) of Irish legend. To confuse matters there is also a derivation from the battle that took place long ago in the mists of time, at the point where three rivers converge – *Áth an Scal*, which means 'Ford of the Heroes'. As a result of these two different accounts of the name, there have been multiple spellings of Annascaul – Anascaul, Annascail, Annasgaul, Anniscail and even Owenascaul, no doubt causing considerable confusion and heated arguments! None-the-less, this is the legend in relation to Scáil, who once lived by the lake, that feeds the river.

*

Fadó, fadó, a long, long time ago, a beautiful, long-haired maiden named Scáil lived alone by the lake at the foot of the mountain pass *Macha na Bó,* between Knockmulanane and Dromavally. Scáil lived happily alone in the forest, living off of the land and drinking from the lake. She was also in the habit of taking a daily bath in the crystal clear waters of the lake, naked as one would expect, given her splendid isolation.

Scáil was perfectly content alone, she did not seek the company of man or woman and remained in perfect solitude until one morning she was rudely interrupted from her daily ablutions by the shouts of a loud voice from high up on

Knockmulanane mountain. Unknown to her, a huge giant had come across the pass and now stood atop the mountain looking down at her and was hurling obscenities at her. Scáil was utterly shocked, not least by the sight of a giant, ogling her in her innocent nakedness, but also by the filthy language and insults that she heard bellowed at her in a huge gruff voice.

Scáil became fearful as she saw the giant make moves to descend from the mountain towards her, but as luck would have it, none other than the Ulster champion Cúchulainn appeared on the opposite mountain, with the two high up on either side of the pass *Macha na Bó*. Cúchulainn, who had not been far off, had run there at great speed, no doubt attracted by the foul-mouthed shouting of the giant.

He immediately began hurling insults and satires at the giant, creating verses off the top of his head to malign the giant's reputation and even questioning his lineage. The giant soon forget all about Scáil and turned his wrath towards Cúchulainn, responding in kind. As the insults flew between the two the tension grew and tempers frayed. Scáil looked on in admiration of this handsome young man who had come to her defence, thankful for being saved from a terrible fate at the hands of the gruesome giant. As the day passed, the verbal conflict became more extreme, until the giant finally lost all self control and began to hurl a huge boulder across the pass at Cúchulainn, which barely missed him. Of course, at this the red mist descended on Cúchulainn and his face and body twisted in rage. Empowered by his rage, Cúchulainn picked up a massive boulder and hurled it back at the giant, beginning a violent exchange of immense stones across from one mountain top to the other.

As the hours passed, the giant boulders flew back and forth while Scáil watched from below. Eventually the giant hit home with a huge rock, that must have weighed twenty tons if it weighed anything at all. Cúchulainn let out a huge cry of pain and disappeared from view. Fortunately it was only a glancing blow to the cheek, but it was sufficient to give considerable pain and to cause Cúchulainn to lose his footing and slip down the mountain a few yards, cursing and grumbling loudly.

All this was unknown to Scáil, who had by now become quite enchanted by Cúchulainn's good looks and bravery against a much larger opponent. When she saw Cúchulainn struck with the boulder, cry out and disappear she let out a cry of despair, believing him crushed to death by the blow.

Distraught by the sudden death of her protector and fearful of her fate, at the hands of the victorious giant, Scáil threw herself into the lake and drowned. Cúchulainn avenged her death, leaping over to the other side of the pass in one bound and crushing the giant's skull with an even larger boulder.

However, in some versions of the story, Cúchulainn died from the giant's blow and so he was buried nearby at the cairns at Dromavally known as the bed, house or grave of Cúchulainn.

The cairns on top of Knockmulanane (which was slightly higher) and Dromavally remain there to this day, as a testament to this great battle. Who actually won the fight remains a mystery and a bone of contention to this day, but regardless of the victor, it was most likely that it is from this sad tale of Scáil that Annascaul takes its name.

A Story of Witchcraft

One morning in May many years ago, a priest near Castlemaine was called out at midnight to attend a dying man in a distant part of the parish. The priest mounted his horse, and after having prepared the sinner he drove off on his homeward journey alone. The greyness of dawn began to appear over the hills and after a time he dismounted and walked slowly on his journey.

The priest then drew his breviary from his pocket and commenced reading his morning prayers. He had not gone far when he noticed his horse trying to stop in the road and getting frightened he looked into a field where there were some cows grazing. He went a little further, and then the horse made a sudden plunge and tried to get away from him and gallop off.

The priest found it hard to hold the horse and he was shaking all over, but after he pulled up the horse, by no means could he move. The priest did not know what to do, and looking around he saw the strangest thing, which made the blood curdle in his veins. It was the legs of a woman from the hips downward, walking up and down the path. The good father was very much alarmed but he resolved to stand firm and take a closer look.

The half body wore yellow buck-skin breeches, fastened at the knees with green ribbons, it had neither shoes nor stockings on, and its legs were covered with long red hairs. The priest examined the legs and spoke to them, but no answer came. He then struck the apparition a blow, after which it made a wild yell and fell to the ground, and the whole place was running over with milk.

The priest was frightened by this, his head swam, and a strange stupor came over him. When he came to, the frightful spectre had vanished and in its place he found an old woman of the neighbourhood, stretched on the road, half drowned in milk. She was noted in the parish for witchcraft, and by requesting help of the devil had assumed the monstrous shape, and was out that morning taking the milk from the cows of the village.

The priest then spoke to her and said "Sarah Kennedy, I have long advised you to give up your evil ways, and now wretched woman you are caught in the midst of your crimes." She groaned and said "Oh Father, Father, can you do anything to save me I am lost." The priest could not reply, shocked at the sight of her face which was as black as night and a short time after she died, right there on the spot. Her remains were removed to her old cabin, and were buried in a sand-pit nearby. She was denied a Christian burial. Her only daughter made her escape and never returned, and her old cabin was burned to the ground.

Based on a story collected by Peggy Kavanagh from William Hanafin (Laharn, Castlemaine)

The Burial Ground (*An Reilig*)

There are three graveyards in the parish. One in Killshanig, one in Killiney and one in Stradbally. There was a graveyard in *Oilean-t-Seannaig*, but it was closed up because in the 16th century a Spanish galleon appeared off *Rinn-no-Fear-Dhearg*. At night time they came to the graveyard with a number of dead men that died of a terrible plague and buried them in there. When they were gone the inhabitants of the island dug up the bodies thinking there would be gold buried with them. But in the morning there was no living person left on the island. They all died of the plague and ever since the graveyard wasn't used.

There are old ruins of churches on the three graveyards. There is a graveyard where protestants were buried in the old ruin in Killiney. There are also a few tombs in the old ruin in Killshanig.

There is an old church on the island, with an altar built of stone - there is a stone in the altar and a cross carved out in it. There is also a stone cross outside the church. This cross was carried to the mainland by men that came to the island, but the following morning the cross was mysteriously found standing back on the island again. There are a few beehive cells on the island also. The graveyard in Killshanig is sloping west and has no trees. The other graveyards are not sloping but they have trees in and around them.

Collected by Cait O'Connor (Na Machair/Magharees)

The Death of Cú Roí (*Aided Con Roí*)

Caher Con Roí, Caherconree, on *Sliabh Mis*, is an ancient fortress two acres in extent, on a triangular spur of the mountain, 2050 feet above sea level. It is protected by two cliffs of 200 feet deep, and it is about 700 feet below the summit, thus making it difficult to attack. The rampart is 350 feet by 14 feet and it is part of one of the three old forts of Erin, along with *Dún Sobhairche* and *Dún Cearnmna*. It must have been built with considerable effort, at such a height, making it a fort of considerable importance in pre-Christian Irish culture, which is, no doubt, why both the fort and Cú Roí are mentioned in so many Irish myths.

In the tale of *Cath Fintraga* it is called *Cathair na Claenraithe*, because of its sloping aspect. Below the fort is an old ogham stone marked *Conuneatt moqi Conuri* and *Fect Cununi*. *Cathair Chonroi* (Caher Con Roí) was built by Ciagdorn, from Cashel, who was fort builder and architect for Cú Roí. Like many other forts of great age, Caherconree is built of uncemented stones, carefully overlapped. Cú/Con Roí is thought to have lived in the first century CE and features in many ancient tales of the Red Branch knights. The *Tuath sen Erann*, or people of old Erin, made *temair Erann* on *Cathair Conraoi,* their headquarters in westen Munster. Cú Roí and his son Lugaid mac Conrói were kings of West Munster, west of a line from Cork to Limerick cities. Lugaid mac Conrói, joined the forces of Queen Maebh in attacking the stricken Ulstermen and it was he who finally slew Cúchulainn, gaining vengance for the death of his father Cú Roí, killed by Cúchulainn's treachery at Cathair Con Roí.

This story is somewhat confused in that elsewhere Cú Roí is given as the father of Blathnaid rather than as her kidnapper and then husband. Blathnaid is given here as daughter of Midir (usually it is Mend), none-the-less the outcome of the story is the same. Another story (The Beheading Test) takes place at Caherconree, where Cú Roí, Blathnaid and Cúchulain are found, along with Laoighre Buadach, Conall Cearnach and the giant Uabh. Elements of this story seem to have found their way into this story of the demise of Cú Roí.

*

Cú Roí MacDáire was the King of Munster and a fearsome warrior with superhuman abilities, magical powers and also a master of disguise. He was the son of Dáire mac Dedad (Dáire Doimthech), and was one of the *Clanna Dedad*.

Cú Roí had a great fort on the Dingle Peninsula, high above the cliffs of the great *Sliabh Mis* mountain range, but he was rarely seen there due to his penchant for traveling all around Ireland and the world. Cú Roí had many enemies and he feared for the safety of his people at his fort on *Sliabh Mis*, that was known as Caherconree. Cú Roí was, through his powerful magic, able make the entire fort spin around at night so that no-one could find its entrance, thereby making the fort invulnerable to attack.

Cú Roí had many adventures, including some with the mighty Ulsterman Cúchulainn of the Red Branch, who became his good friend. One time, Cúchulainn was visiting a friend across the water in fair *Cymru* when he met Cú Roí drinking in one of the dark and damp hostelries there. He bade Cúchulainn to sit and join him for a drink and they chatted for some time about their land and peoples. As time passed Cúchulainn told Cú Roí "I wish to go on a raid of the otherword beyond the great veil and I would like you to join me and you will have first choice in the spoils of this raid." Cú Roí was delighted when he heard of the potential rewards, so he eagerly agreed and set about preparing for their venture.

The two heroes met at the entrance to the otherworld near *Cruacháin*, and with their men, one by one they filed down through into the otherworld realm. A great slaughter ensued in the otherworld, but through Cú Roí's and Cúchulainn's bravery, they were triumphant. The victorious heroes returned to the world of men and carried off the spoils of battle: Midir's cauldron of plenty, his magical cows and his daugher, Blathnaid.

As they emerged back outside the rath, Cú Roí placed his hand on Blathnaid and said "this will be my payment, and I shall take her as my wife." but the Ulstermen said that he could have nothing and they all began to laugh at him.

In anger Cú Roí picked up all the spoils as well as Blathnaid and began to walk off when Cúchulainn stood up and placed his open hand on Cú Roí's chest to stop him from leaving. Cúchulainn was then picked up with one hand by Cú Roí and flung back down to the ground with such force that he found himself buried in soil up to his armpits. If this were not undignified enough, Cú Roí took his sword and sliced off the locks from Cúchulainn's head, which was a grave insult to any man. None of the other

Red Branch knights tried to intervene for fear of Cú Roí, who returned home unabated.

Cúchulainn was so shamed by losing his hair that he went into exile and hid from his fellow men for a year and a day until his hair had grown back. He vowed revenge for the great insult, and so schemed to visit Cú Roí's new wife, Blathnaid at the fort Caherconree on the *Sliabh Mis* mountain, while Cú Roí was away.

Although Blathnaid became the queen of *Cathair Chonroi* and was treated well by her husband, the fort Caherconree was a forbidding and lonely place as the fort was on top of a high peak. It is said Bláthnad taunted Cú Roí that his fort was too small for such a magnificent chieftain's wife to live in and so he flew into a rage and tore down his walls to build a bigger fort, that would be worthy of his bride. Blathnaid was still very angry at being taken from her otherworld home and being forced to marry against her will, so she was happy to agree to Cúchulainn's overtures despite his part in her kidknapping.

Cúchulainn and Blathnaid soon became lovers and together they plotted the murder of Cú Roí, so that they could be together unhindered. However, Cú Roí was not an easy man to kill because his soul rested (in the form of an apple) in the stomach of a salmon, living in a stream in the *Sliabh Mis* mountains. His wife had learned the secret of his mortality by constantly flattering her husband, Cú Roí, who had boasted of his indestructibility. Blathnaid bid Cúchulainn to leave and await Cú Roí returning home to Caherconree. However, before returning to kill Cú Roí he must first find and kill the magical salmon, otherwise he would be unable to slay Cú Roí. She warned him to wait for her signal - when the stream below Caherconree turned white from milk poured into it then he should come back.

Cúchulainn eventually found the salmon and caught it, cutting open its stomach to remove the apple that contained Cú Roí's soul, which he crushed into the ground. Cúchulainn waited at the stream below the great fort of Caherconree as the day began to darken, waiting for a signal from Blathnaid so that he could enter the castle while Cú Roí lay asleep and slay him.

Balthnaid distracted Cú Roí so that he forgot to enchant the fortress to spin at nightfall and after he was sound asleep she poured gallons of milk into a stream which flowed out near the entrance to the castle. Cúchulainn saw her signal and raced up, found the entrance soon enough and Blathnaid led him to her husband's bedroom. Cúchulainn murdered Cú Roí with his sword as the great sorcerer, warrior and king lay sleeping peacefully in his bed.

The two lovers, Cúchulainn and Blathnaid made good their escape by running across the battlements of the castle. However, the Druid Ferchertne, always loyal to Cú Roí, guessed what had happened when he saw Cúchulainn and Blathnaid fleeing the castle at speed. Ferchertne gave chase and quickly grabbed Blathnaid, with both of his arms around her and hurled himself from the cliff top, as reward for her cruel betrayal of her husband. Cúchulainn, powerless to prevent the tragedy unfolding, watched in horror as Blathnaid and Ferchertne fell to a gruesome death on the rocks below.

Landlordism on the Dingle Peninsula

The Great O' Connell, in his great aggregate meetings through-out Ireland, always concluded his speech with the remark: "This is a great day for Ireland but I think there was never a greater day came in this country, than the day the Land Purchase Schemes were introduced and carried into effect."

Landlordism was the after effect of the English conquest of Ireland. The favourites of the Lord Deputies, or the Court, or those who distinguished themselves in the slaughter of the unarmed Irish, were granted huge tracts of land, to which they had no God-given right, but the right of the strong man against the weaker man.

Thus, we have one Edward Denny granted 6000 acres of splendid land all around the town of Tralee, from which the Irish peasant was driven away, into the mountains, and to the bogs of the Dingle Peninsula. So it was, also with the Herberts of Cahirnan, Muckross and Killeetierna. The Browns (Lord Kenmare), De Moleyns and hundreds of others were granted thousands of acres of land, to which they had no real claim, but by the sword.

In fact one Lord Deputy was perfecting a scheme, by which to drive the Irish peasant out of the country altogether, and between the slaughter of the unfortunate people, and the famine (that was brought on by the potato blight), there is hardly any doubt, but he would have succeeded if allowed to implement it. However, those large estates hung heavy in the hands of those who stole them from the native Irish. They had no-one to work them, and there was no revenue coming from the thousands of acres of confiscated lands, without the help of the native Irish to work the land.

Many of the new owners wanted money to spend in England, for they had little or no enjoyment in this country to suit them. So the Lord Deputy abandoned his scheme, and the Irish were enticed out of the bogs and glens of the mountains, and given small portions of their own land, at an enormous rent, fixed by the new landlords. The poor people were glad of any concession they could obtain, so they gladly went to work to try to make money for the landlords to spend on frivolity in Dublin, London, Paris and other such places.

Anywhere from six to ten pounds per plot was reckoned as a reasonable rent, and rent proved handy when more money was wanted, to help the landlords refill their coffers, after the excesses and debauchery of Dublin, London, Paris, Berlin or even the Grand Tour of the Mediterranean. The order would be sent back to Ireland, by cash starved landlords, to raise the rent at once and the next thing to occur was that the tenants had notice from the Estate Bailiff or Driver (as he was then called), that the rent had been raised. Tenants had to be prepared to meet the extra expense at once, as the landlords wanted money immediately and would not be kept waiting. Failure to pay up led to eviction of tenants by force. Some schemes created by landlords (such as Lord Ventry) did enable some of the poor to earn money by building pointless follies around Dingle, but these only helped a limited number of people, for a fairly short period of time.

The poor people, in order to meet the demands of rent, were in a great many cases forced to live on mainly potatoes, and milk twice a day, or even just one daily. Generally they could not afford to eat more than twice a day, and even less so during the famine times. Many of the people went away out of these lands by foot, and carried with them what little possessions they had, most never to return. Others saved the fare or sold all they had to buy passage to America or Australia and begin a new life. However, as one man said, many of the tenants died of starvation, bravely trying to pay the rent, although some, who were in a relatively prosperous position, succeeded in keeping their tenancy and avoided facing the horrors of hunger.

England was on bad terms with much of Europe and America too and so had nowhere convenient to turn to for extra food, except for Ireland. As a result, Irish butter, wheat, barley, vegetables, beer, beef, bacon and eggs were flooding the English markets, exported from Ireland. Meanwhile, the Irish people struggled to survive, or worse still, they were forced to emigrate or otherwise face death by starvation.

Based on a story collected by Peggy Kavanagh from William Hanafin (Laharn, Castlemaine)

A Ghost Story

A good many years ago there was a man named Seán who lived on the mountain-side west of Dingle. He lived with his wife and his mother in a nice tidy house and a small farm, on which he kept two or three cows.

Seán was a strong able man and a good workman, but he had one great fault; he was very fond of playing cards at night and often went five miles away from home to play in local card games. One night, he was out playing very late at a farmer's house, a good distance away from home. They were playing long after twelve o'clock and finally the farmer said it was time to go home now and so up he got.

Seán got his stick and fastened his cap on his head and off he went in the dark, back towards his own home. About half way home he came to the church and a burial ground on the roadside but there was a high wall between it and the road. As he approached, Seán heard some great noise coming from around one of the tombs.

He stopped and looked into the graveyard and he saw a black man scraping at a grave. Seán jumped in over the wall and waving his stick firmly, cried out "Who are you? If you are a dead man I will pray for you, but if you are a living man I will give you some of this." brandishing his stick.

"I am neither one nor the other!" said the black man.

"And what are you then?" said Seán, showing not the slightest worry.

"Well" said he, "I am the old boy."

"Yerra begor," said Seán "I was after wishing to meet you to have a chat with you, so now come on home with me. I will give you a night's lodgings and you will be well treated besides."

"Why do you ask me to go with you?" said the dark figure.

"Well my lad," said Seán "I will tell you. I have your younger sister, my wife, at home for many years."

"Thank you, but go home now." said the ghostly man, "I never met a man like you before."

So Seán went home and slept well - as soundly as a baby, despite it all. He told his wife and mother and all those who had a mind to listen the story. All were mightily impressed and thereafter he was always called "*Seán gan Eagla*" (Sean without fear).

Based on a story collected by John Joe Shea from John McCarthy (Castlemaine)

The Story of Muirisín

Long ago there lived a little man called Muirisín at the foot of the Slieve Mish mountains, north-west of Castlemaine. He was a small man but very crafty. Muirisín possessed a nice tidy little cabin and a small farm on which he kept two cows.

He dreamt, three nights in succession, that there were crocks of gold hidden near a bridge in the vicinity of Tipperary town, so Muirisín decided to travel all the way to Tipperary and look for the hidden treasure. When he reached the place that he dreamt of he failed to find the gold, and for some time he spent his days walking along the bridge looking in vain for some clue which would enable him find the treasure that he was in search of.

At last he made up his mind to turn homewards; it was a long journey in those days when there were no motor cars, bicycles or any other modern methods of travel. He was about to leave for home when a man from the town came up to him and said:

"My friend I have seen you on this bridge for three days and I should like to know why you linger here."

"Well dear Sir," replied Muirisín "I dreamt that there was gold hidden near this bridge."

"Very well" replied the stranger "I shall help you."

He searched with Muirisín for the gold but they still failed to find it. He then told Muirisín that he had a dream that if he were in Kerry and in the haggard of a man named Muirisín who lived near Castlemaine, he would find the gold. Muirisín went home, bringing the man from Tipperary with him and when he reached the destination he dug for the gold in the haggard, and to his great joy he found it. Muirisín bought a large property for his sons, gave a portion of the gold to the Tipperary man, who went back home delighted, and Muirisín lived a long comfortable life and died a happy death at home in his simple cabin.

Based on a story collected by Peggy Kavanagh from John McCarthy (Castlemaine)

The Dunquin Castastrophe

Dunquin (*Dún Chaoin*) is a small coastal village to the west of Dingle town. On May 5th 1870, a terrible tragedy unfolded, a couple of miles south-west of Dunquin village, within the parish, at Ballyickeen (*Baile Ícín*).

On the night of May 5th a local fishing vessel that had been collecting seaweed for manure happened across a barrel floating in the sea near Beginish Island. The boatmen brought it on board and returned with it to the house of one of the boatmen (Timothy Crohan) at *Tigh Thaidhg* in Ballyickeen.

At the house, the barrel was opened and found to contain paraffin (also reported as petroleum in some accounts), which was duly divided between the people who found it. Crohan apparently had objected to dividing up the barrel that night, believing it to be too dangerous and he had wanted to leave it until the morning. However, he was swayed by the others present, leading to a disastrous outcome.

Once the barrel was drained and almost empty, one of the party decided to look in the bottom of the barrel using a rush light to see better. Of course, a spark fell from the rush light and ignited what paraffin was left in the barrel, the paraffin spilled on the floor and also the surrounding vessels that the paraffin had been poured into.

The resulting catastrophe was a massive explosion within the house that blew it up and all thirteen people (seven men and six women) and a donkey and two pigs, that were present at the time.

Four people were instantly incinerated where they stood, while the others were all burned to varying degrees as the donkey had blocked escaping via the only doorway. Meanwhile, the survivors of the initial blast were burned further, as the burning thatch roof fell in on them, hemmed in by the donkey still preventing their escape.

After the survivors eventually emerged, local physician Dr Hudson was called to the scene, where three survivors were so badly burned that they were not expected to recover. In total, seven died as a result of the explosion – Tom Long, his wife Léan Long (formerly Moran), Kate Daly, Micheál Daly, Máire Tadhg Óg Crohan, Cait Tadhg Óg Crohan and Eibhlís Tadhg Óg Crohan.

Four had died immediately, and the remaining nine people who had been in the house were badly burned, with three more dying within a week. All six who survived were badly burned, with some having to have their clothes cut off with a knife. Timothy Crohan and his wife Caít Crohan, who owned the house, were among the six survivors of the terrible fire, but their three daughters sadly perished.

Some of the victims removed from the house were incomplete and buried with missing limbs, also some body parts that were recovered from the wreck of the house, were buried in the nearby graveyard without coffins, as it was unknown to whom they belonged.

The news caused great upset and a sensation throughout Kerry and it was reported in the Kerry and Cork newspapers. The then unknown Peig Sayers (born 1873), heard the story from her mother when she was a teenager, and recorded the terrible incident in her now famous autobiography, *Peig - A Scéal Féin*.

Timothy Crohan, for obvious reasons, did not wish to rebuild the house and hoped to move to a new location to start again. He was a tenant of Lord Ventry, whose agent promised to rebuild the house. So, Crohan walked the nine miles to Lord Ventry's home in Dingle, where after waiting a whole day for an audience, he was told that the best he could be offered was to live rent free for one year.

After pressure from the local community and with winter fast approaching, Crohan eventually relented and built a new house on the site of the old one that had burned down. Members of the Crohan and Moriarty families continued to live in the new house until 1975. Later the house was restored and a ruined outbuilding was rebuilt and added as a second house by Bob Landers, a local builder. The two houses are still standing, having been sold on, and are occupied to this day.

The Dwarf and the Piper

There was a dwarf living near *Lios na h-Adairce* long ago. He was living nearby the village, under the ground and he was an enchanted fellow, as is to be expected of such creatures. There was a man living not far away from the dwarf and he was a piper, but in truth a very poor one. The dwarf hated the noise of the uilleann pipes, which sounded more like a cat being strangled, such was the poor quality of the playing. None-the-less, the piper used go about every day playing his pipes and thereby vexing the poor dwarf, who was a lover of good music.

This particular day, the dwarf came out from his underground lair and the piper was playing as usual and he said to him that that was a nice tune and that he would like to hear it again. The piper was much surprised but the piper played on and the dwarf told him to come in to his dwelling afterwards for the chat and a smoke.

He went in and the dwarf told him that one of the local chiefs would be getting married and there would be a great feast. He said to the piper that they would go to the feast, but to this the piper said that they would be shot with arrows or worse still, a musket, if they were to be seen there, as they were not invited.

To this the dwarf replied that it would be no bother at all, as he had two magic cloaks, and "if you had them on you, you would be invisible" he said to the incredulous piper. And so they went to the feast dressed in their invisible cloaks and they carried with them two big bags to bring away a good load of whatever they should choose to take.

They went into the chief's great house and jumped up onto the long table and started filling up their bags. The guests at the feast saw the silver platters and the fine food disappearing before their very eyes and so many of the people became frightened and many said that there must be some evil spirits around the place.

The dwarf pulled off the cloak from the piper all of a sudden and the people immediately saw him, leapt upon him and caught him. The poor piper, who had been tricked, was brought before the chief and it was decided that he should be hanged the next morning at sunrise. However, the chief's men wanted to return to the celebrations, and as they had a big thick rope handy they used it to tie the distraught piper tightly to a tree, just outside the chief's great house.

The dwarf was delighted to see the piper suffer, as revenge for the terrible music that had been inflicted on him. However, when he heard that the piper was to be put to death he felt sorry for him and thought better of his vengeful actions. Under his invisible cloak, the dwarf sneaked up to the tree where the piper stood sobbing and he cut the rope quietly.

Next, he whispered into the piper's ear and he told him not to be afraid. Then the dwarf pulled the rope away and it fell to the ground, leaving the piper free to escape, as there were no guards about – they were inside getting drunk. Now the dwarf had kept a hold of the piper's cloak and so he threw the cloak over him and the two of them ran away with their haul of fine bread and foreign wines, the best of meat, silver platters and everything else they had got at.

The two returned home no longer as enemies but as friends, the piper forgave the dwarf for his rotten trick and even took up music lessons so that he might not further disturb the poor dwarf's sensitive ears!

Based on a story collected by B. Ní Iarflatha from Séan Ó Cuire (*An Cam/ Camp*)

Star Wars Comes to Dingle

After the *Star Wars* series was scheduled for another three movies, creator George Lucas and the *Star Wars* team began looking for iconic locations on which to shoot sections of the story. As we now know, they fell in love with Skellig Michael, off the coast of the Dingle Peninsula, and chose it as one of the key locations for the films part VII through to IX.

The final parts of *Star Wars VII: The Force Awakens* were filmed over a three day period on Skellig Michael at the start of the 2014 visitors season. During the winter the sea is so rough that it is often impossible to travel to the island by boat, or even helicopter, so it was necessary to wait for the summer weather. The crew came and went over 2 seasons, according to local guide Catherine Merrigan, but the actual filming itself took place over just three days. The whole *Star Wars* operation took place in total secrecy, with the Irish navy being deployed to keep unscheduled tourist boats and the paparazzi away from the island during filming.

Towards the end of the 2015 filming, the cast and crew spent an evening in The Courthouse Pub (in Dingle), which was attended by this book's illustrator Elena Danaan, during which time she met most of the main actors and many of the production's crew.

Lucafilm returned to the Dingle area in 2016 for *Star Wars VIII: The Last Jedi*, much of which was filmed at *Ceann Sibéal* (Sibeal Head), situated at the western tip of the Dingle Peninsula. A replica of the 'Jedi village' of Skellig Michael was constructed at the top of Sibeal Head, along with a life-size Millennium Falcon space-ship. The entire area was closed off to the public, with 24-hour security preventing both the press and the public from getting within a few miles of the filming location. The author was able to view the film set from a distance with binoculars, but even so there was very little to be viewed, due to the thorough security precautions. Footage was also shot for the final part of the trilogy: *Star Wars IX: The Rise Of Skywalker*, but most of it was filmed in 2018 at Pinewood Studios in England.

At the end of filming, in May 2016, the cast and crew went out again in Dingle, for one last hooley at Foxy John's pub on the Main Street of Dingle. During their night out, the stars and crew mingled with a few select locals and Daisy Ridley (who played lead character 'Rey') even got to have a go at pulling pints, during an especially busy period.

Talking to Jimmy Fallon for *VIP* magazine, Daisy revealed her bartending prowess: "The thing is, not to float my own boat, but I'm a really good bartender. I worked in two different pubs for like a year and a half, in a rowdy London district just before *Star Wars*."

"I'm a good bartender so I worked the wrap party. It was just, there was a big queue, and I was like 'Hey guys, can I get back there?' And I did, and it was fantastic!" Daisy revealed.

Foxy John's pub would not generally have world-famous film stars serving the customers, or be willing to accommodate four-legged customers, but they made an exception for Mark Hamill (who played Luke Skywalker) who had brought along his wee dog Millie.

Not long after the wrap party, another unexpected *Star Wars* happening hit the peninsula. On the Monday 23rd May the pupils of *Scoíl an Fheitearaigh* (Ballyferriter primary school) gave a recital of the *Star Wars* Imperial March on tin whistles and accordions. Unknown to the children, a surprise visitor, from a far-away galaxy was soon to make an appearance! They had been told to expect a special guest for the performance, but the 65 pupils were all totally stunned to see none other than Chewbacca, co-pilot of the Millennium Falcon, walk into their classroom.

Pupil Oísin Ó Fearghail, aged 9, said that "He lifted up a few of the kids and he gave me a hug!"

"He stayed for over half an hour and he could understand us, but we couldn't understand Shyriiwook." said another pupil, Ruadhán Ó Dálaigh, aged 8.

The entire school was photographed with their 8-foot tall VIP alien visitor, with one lucky boy, Cillian Ó Baoil, appearing in Chewbacca's arms for the front cover of *The Irish Examiner* national paper, a couple of days later.

Unfortunately, the set on Sibeal Head was totally dismantled and taken away, but even so, Dingle has since become very much a place of pilgrimage for *Star Wars* fans from all over the world. On every May 4th both Dingle town and Ballyferriter host the "May The Fourth Be With You" *Star Wars* festival.

The Dead Man's Height or the Glen of Scotia

Away to the north west of the Mall, in the townland of Boolteens, and the parish of Keel, lies a little hilltop called Hill of the Dead (*Cnoc na Marb*) very little at present is known about this little hill or height and there is no interest taken in it, yet according to the old history of Kerry, and also to tradition, a great battle was fought there many hundreds of years ago. The battle was one of vital importance for the people of Ciar (Ciar being the son of Fergus mac Róich). It was in memory of Ciar (*Ciarraighe/ Ciarraí*) that county Kerry derives its name.

The invaders were thought to be Scots or Milesians, who at a later time peopled Scotland. Their forces made a descent on this island, probably with the intention of establishing a colony, because they were accompanied by their queen who was known as Scotia, that they became known as Scots.

They were a brave and hardy race, and it seems they were suited for the purpose of colonisation or plunder. They ravaged the country before the invasion and secured a great deal of captives and plunder in doing so. The *Tuatha Dé Danann* were the rulers in this country at that time, and were not so robust or powerful a fighting force as the Milesians, yet they were their superiors in craft, cunning and magical arts.

They engaged the invaders in or about this hill, and the battle lasted all day. The battle must have extended farther back than the hilltop, for a very few years ago, arrows were found at the west of the road, leading across the mountain to Camp and these are at present in the museum in Dublin. These arrows were found more plentifully around a height and on the far side of it, which shows that the invaders either entered at or took over the far side of the height.

Farther down on the level ground, stone hatchets were found, very probably the engagement here was hand to hand combat. The *Tuatha Dé Danann* got the best of the fighting for it seems they used the black arts or magic as, according to tradition, they were masters at that business. The Milesians had to flee and were killed in large numbers along the mountain side. Kerry's tradition has it that queen Scotia and her ladies, seeing the slaughter of their countrymen, raised a great cry (*Caoine*) for the dead, a practice (keening) that continued long afterwards into modern times.

It is said that the great cry was the foundation of that exquisite air which is played on the fiddle called *Sliabh na mban* (Slievenamon). At this time very few players ever heard of it, yet it was remembered by an old man named Michael Hurley, who was a great musician, and people say that at certain times and places he would play it in a darkened room with a large key attached to the fiddle.

At any rate, the Milesians were mostly killed. Their queen, Scotia and her ladies including the lady Fas, who was a lady of Grecian extraction and of great beauty, were killed in that lonely mountain pass which still bears her name - *Gleann Scotín* or Scotia's Glen.

Her grave is still known to this day. A good many years ago, when Kerry were a hurling team second to none, I [William

Hanafin] was crossing the mountain to see a hurling match between Kerry and Limerick. Going down towards Clahane Bridge, I was surprised to see a crowd of about twenty people coming up the mountain. They were Limerick people coming to Foley's Wood, to see the grave of Scotia and one of the party accosted me and told me where they were going. I gave them all the information I possessed on the place.

Based on a story collected by Peggy Kavanagh from William Hanafin (Laharn, Castlemaine). Note: *Sliabh na mBan* is generally regarded as as in Tipperary, it is possible the collector meant *Sliabh Mis*, which is close to where Scotia's Grave is located.

Ryan's Daughter (High Jinx & Big Money Come to Dingle)

Dingle was not so long ago a bit of a backwater, a small fishing town, pretty much unknown outside of Kerry. This all changed in February 1969 when world famous film director David Lean brought his crew and cast to Dingle to film *Ryan's Daughter*. The film was the beginning of Dingle's rejuvenation, but one of the main reasons that the film was made in Dingle was that the lead actress, Sarah Miles, couldn't bear to be away from her four dogs and was reluctant to travel anywhere that would require her to put her dogs into quarantine. Robert Bolt's (the script writer) original idea was to make a film version of the book *Madame Bovary*, starring his wife, actress Sarah Miles. David Lean read the script and not liking it much, suggested that Bolt rework it into another setting. The film script was changed, but it retains parallels with Flaubert's novel – Rosy parallels Emma Bovary, Charles is her husband, Major Doryan is analogous to Rodolphe and Leon, Emma's lovers. Lean's two right-hand men, Peter Dukelow (construction) and Eddie Fowlie (location), took a look at Sicily, Sardinia and the Shetland Isles before finally settling on the Dingle Peninsula. And so, Robert Bolt rewrote the script and the whole story was transported to the west of Ireland.

Various famous actors were considered for roles, such as Alec Guinness (who turned down Father Collins), Paul Scofield, George C. Scott, Anthony Hopkins, Marlon Brando, Patrick McGoohan, Gregory Peck, Richard Burton, Richard Harris and Peter O'Toole. In the end Robert Mitchum was chosen to play

Charles Shaughnessy, but he was reluctant at first, due to a personal crisis, however in the end he agreed to the role and to filming in Ireland.

The film, released in 1970, grossed nearly $31 million and was allocated what at the time was a staggering budget of $9.5 million. Originally the film was scheduled to shoot over a matter of months, but it overran by 135 days and was $3,549,833 over budget, giving an overall cost of $13.3 million. As a result of a troublesome cast and bad weather delays, filming took a year and almost two years in total to film, edit and prepare for its commercial release. By the time location shooting ended, on 24th February 1970, an entire year after commencing, £1m to £3m (punts) had been spent in the Dingle area.

New cars, house extensions, new kitchens and bathrooms began to appear among a populace that had been rapidly introduced to 20th century consumerism, due to the largesse of David Lean and his crew. One local hardware shop was used to selling 1 or 2 gas heaters (such as the Superser) per year, but as the crew and cast were often complaining of the cold and windy weather, Lean ordered over a dozen gas heaters to keep his people warm - a single purchase that made the shop owner a small fortune! The pubs were generally full, due to the large crew and also the extra money earned by locals who were working on the film. Pretty much every guesthouse on the peninsula did roaring business during the filming, as it was a huge production and everyone working on it needed accommodation.

Many stories are remembered by locals to this day, with rowdy actor Robert Mitchum featuring most colourfully in many of them. Mitchum was installed in Milltown House hotel, only a very short walk from Dingle town, which he referred to as 'house arrest'. It is reputed that the road leading down to the hotel was nearly worn away by the trail of young women and drinking pals making their way to see Mitchum, who was a well-known womaniser, with a fondness for hard liquor and marijuana. Who knows how many of Dingle's sons and daughter are actually the progeny of the infamous actor Robert Mitchum? More than one or two is quite likely! The Miltown House hotel today is still very popular with tourists and it has a bar lounge named after him and pictures of Mitchum, from the time, decorate the walls of the hotel.

Mitchum eventually moved into a rented house, which Sarah Miles described as the 'Dingle Brothel', and Mitchum loved to invite both the film crew and Dingle locals to his home, where he would often serve them hash browns and burgers, no doubt washed down with copious amounts of booze and marijuana cigarettes. Speaking about her co-star, Sarah Miles (who had an affair with him some time after the film) had this to say of Robert Mitchum:

"I never smoked before I met him, I was so innocent you know. I was supposedly an icon of the 60s and I'd never smoked in my life, I never even drank and he corrupted me."

As well as hard drinking, Mitchum was known for getting into fights, most often when a good deal of drink had been taken - following one drunken brawl, he had to endure a three-week lay-off due to a massive black eye making filming his scenes impossible.

One story of Robert Mitchum involved local dairy farmer Stevie Kelleher, who was bringing his cows down the road, very near to Miltown House hotel. Mitchum was in his car and being held up by the cows was rather annoyed. He shouted out to Kelleher to hurry up, adding "Do you know who I am? I'm Robert Mitchum!"

Kelleher had never heard of Mitchum and replied "I don't care if you're Robert Emmet!" (the 18th century Irish rebel leader) and continued on at his own pace, to Mitchum's obvious displeasure.

Mitchum often clashed with director David Lean, saying that "Working with David Lean is like constructing the Taj Mahal out of toothpicks." Despite the difficult working relationship and Mitchum's well-known fondness for drinking and mayhem, the film was completed successfully, going on to later become regarded as a masterpiece. Mitchum, despite his personal dislike of him, acknowledged that Lean was one of the best directors he had worked with during his long career. Mitchum, some time after the release of the film, confided to friends and family that *Ryan's Daughter* was one of his best roles and that he regretted the negative critical response the film received at the time. However, despite some bad reviews, it was popular with the viewing public and turned a tidy profit for Metro-Goldwyn-Mayer and Faraway Productions, although it was far less successful than Lean's previous film *Doctor Zhivago*.

As part of the production, an entire fake village was constructed, which was later dismantled by Kerry County Council, in the belief that it might attract drug addicts or homeless people, however it would have made a very viable tourist attraction had it been kept! The film set village of Kirrary had to be built from scratch, in the hills behind Dunquin, using local workmen to do all of the work. In 1969 the average industrial wage was between £6 and £7 (punts) per week, but the workers involved in creating the pretend village were able to earn up to £40 a week.

The only remaining building from the *Ryan's Daughter* film is the school house, located next to Gobnait's Well, overlooking the Atlantic just outside of Dunquin (*Dún Chaoin*). Unfortunately, the building is now in terrible condition, with the roof completely collapsed in and gone – only the windowless walls of the building remain. Without major restoration this last remnant of the film will eventually collapse, which would be a great pity – it is after all part of the legacy of *Ryan's Daughter*, the film that really put Dingle on the map and kick-started the tourist industry here.

More than three decades after *Ryan's Daughter* was filmed in Dingle, Sarah Miles returned to open the very first Dingle International Film Festival in 2006. She returned again in March 2016, ten years later, for a special St. Patrick's Day showing of the film, as part of the 10th Dingle International Film Festival, which took place in The Phoenix Cinema owned by the O'Sullivan family. Sarah Miles was also back in county Kerry to make a documentary on the film, which has long ago passed into both local and cinematic history.

Speaking about how the area had changed since her last visit, Sarah Miles said:

"I was quite stunned when I came back 10 years ago to see how much thoughtless building there was. It upset me to see these thoughtless bungalows all over the place. It's heartbreaking that you can ruin a view with bungalows like that... It's absolutely heartbreaking that it could happen to the most beautiful isle on Earth."

Of course, despite the new houses and inevitable modernisation, Dingle continues to be a major draw for tourists, because of the beautiful scenery, the friendly people, the late dolphin Fungie and undoubtedly the three world-famous films made here, *Star Wars (VII-IX)*, *Far and Away* and the one that started it all – *Ryan's Daughter.*

Loch a'Dúin

The *Loch a'Dúin* valley runs along the northern side of the mountain range running from the Connor Pass eastwards along much of the Dingle Peninsula and within it lies the loch itself, which is long and thin, with a small island in the middle of it. The valley is one thousand five hundred acres in size and passes through three townlands. This area of the Dingle Peninsula has definitely been occupied since the end of the Neolithic period, from about 2500 BCE onwards, which becomes clear from all the remains of former habitation.

Today the valley is populated mostly by sheep and cows, but in former times it was full of human settlements, from the late stone age, through to almost modern times. There are over eighty stone structures in the valley, which includes two standing stones, a wedge tomb, two cist graves, eleven stones with cup and circle rock art, several raths or enclosures, many huts/*clochaina*, eight *fluachta fiadh* (hot water cooking pits) and even a fortified island. Some of these sites are reputed to have belonged to the *Tuatha Dé Danann*, but this is more tradition than based on any empirical evidence.

With the expansion of the bog over the last three or four thousand years, many of the ancient buildings and walls are buried or partially buried by peat, but this has also served to preserve these ancient sites. It is only relatively recently, due to farmers digging and drying peat, that some of these places have been rediscovered. In some cases the peat has proven useful as pollen samples can be used give an approximate date – for instance excavations in recent decades have revealed stone work of at least two thousand years old, using this technique.

An ancient wedge tomb, with rock art, from perhaps 2500 BCE can be found here, as can two standing stones oriented towards the sunset facing Mount Brandon and this hillock was enclosed by walls, probably as a ritual area, for following the seasonal religious practices of the Neolithic people. Here we find the mysterious rock art with cups cut in the rock as well as circles and spirals. Some speculate that these were used for blood sacrifices or symbolically but we have no way of confirming anything.

As well as ancient human habitation this valley is home to rare plants and flowers, some of which (such as purple flowering Greater Butterwort/*Leith Uisce*) have disappeared from most of Ireland. In the loch itself lies the fortified island in the middle of the lake. which is now home to mute swans instead of people. The remains of dry stone walls and wooden palisades in the water can still be seen from the ancient fortifications. In local legend the island is known as the home of Oscar, the son of Oisín, and grandson of Fionn mac Cumhaill, who reputedly fought in a great battle on the southern side of the peninsula at Ventry beach.

Peig Sayers - Fionn in Search of Youth

Peig Sayers (1873- 1958) is known throughout Ireland for her 1936 *Gaeilge* autobiography *Peig - A Scéal Féin*, which became a standard text in most schools across the country – loved by many but also hated by many school children, who found the recollections of island life by an old woman to be deadly boring! Big Peig or *Peig Mhór* was famed on Great Blasket (*An Blascaod Mór*) as one of the greatest story tellers in the Irish language, leading to many visits from folklore collectors to hear her speak.

Peig was born at Dunquin (*Dún Chaoin*) in 1873, but moved to Great Blasket when she married fisherman Pádraig Ó Guithín in 1892. From the late 1930s onwards her stories were collected by the Irish Folklore Commission, with over 400 items being written down from her orations. She lived on Great Blasket (*An Blascaod Mór*) until 1942, when she returned to her home village of Dunquin, but she was moved to St Anne's Hospital in Dublin, due to cancer treatment, but she was eventually moved to St Elizabeth's Hospital in Dingle, where she remained until her death in 1958. Peig was buried in the Dunquin burial ground, but she will forever be associated with the Blasket Islands and attempts to preserve and encourage the use of *Gaeilge*, the Irish language.

In 1952, when she was in St. Anne's Hospital (in Dublin), being treated for cancer, a series of gramophone recordings were made of 9 folk tales, an oral history of life on the Blasket Islands (*Na Blascaodaí*) and various prayers, all *as Gaeilge*. This collection was much later translated into English but some of her collected stories were published in 1957, a year prior to her death. However, the project to publish her complete recordings, transcribed in both Irish and English, did not come to fruition until 2020, delayed due to the unfortunate death of editor Bo Almqvist, in 2013.

As well as the transcripts, the book *Peig Sayers: Níl Deireadh Ráite* includes 2 CDs of the remastered original recordings, enabling us to listen to Peig's stories in her own words, almost as if we are sat in the room with her! Although the author's grasp of Irish is basically that of a 5 year-old, to listen to Peig during the writing and transcribing of this particular story was both haunting and inspiring – it being quite surprising how clear, even paced and easy on the ear her voice and delivery was.

This particular story, from the St. Anne's Hospital recordings, was regarded as one of Peig's favourite stories, as it has been told by her and transcribed by folklorists at various times previous to this version. This version, presented, here is taken from the audio recording and was translated into English for the Irish Folklore Commission, by Seán Ó Súilleabháin (1903-1996) who worked extensively on Peig's collected material. This translation of the tale was originally published by New Island Books in *Peig Sayers: Níl Deireadh Ráite*, edited by Bo Almqvist & Pádraig Ó Héalaí.

*

Fionn and some of his warriors were hunting and giving chase one day in a place that was far away from habitation. It so happened as the day wore on, that a fog came down and was so thick about them that they couldn't tell east from west. As they peered about, trying to make their way, they thought they saw a bothy ahead of them, a hovel – you know – on the wayside where it wasn't seen before that. But they knew nothing about it as they were all, every one of them, so enveloped in fog that they couldn't see beyond their own shoes.

However, they approached the house and went inside and as they did they sat themselves down on seats here and there. There was nobody in the house when they came in but an extremely old man, ridden with rheumatic pains, covered in body hair and whiskers with a long flowing mane. I imagine that even Conán was frightened when he saw his appearance. A fine slip of a young beautiful girl was busy with the household chores and as soon as she completed preparing food for the Fianna, she disappeared into an adjoining room.

Sean Ó Súilleabháin (the recorder): I see.

Because it seems the Fianna were full of devilment – they were all trying to outwit each other in their eagerness to be close to the young woman, to have some fun with her and enjoy her company and conversation. However, she kept away from them. She prepared the dinner then laid out the table for them and had placed chairs and everything in a fitting and proper manner as a servant in a royal court of this kind would do for nobles.

There was what looked like a big strong wether (castrated ram) tied by some kind of chain to the far wall of the house. But when the men had sat down at the table, this wether sprang up, broke loose from the tie on its neck and attacked the table.

SÓS: I see.

He turned it upside down and scattered all the food and drink that was on it.

"Tether the sheep, Conán." Said Fionn.

Fionn, or rather Conán, got up and went and caught the sheep by the ear and dragged it to the post where it was tethered. But even if he had twenty more such as himself to help him, he couldn't tether the sheep. Each one of the Fianna who accompanied Fionn tried to tether the sheep but none of them was able to do it.

In the end, they were hungry and annoyed with the situation. They couldn't sit at the table, for as soon as the food was placed on it ready to be eaten, the brute of a sheep turned it upside down...

SÓS: On the floor.

On the floor. Finally, a voice spoke to this old man who had spent all his life in the corner:

"Tether the sheep, you decrepit fellow."

SÓS: I see.

He got up and when he left his nook in the ashes, almost seven pounds of ash fell from the seat of his trousers – he had spent such a length of time there himself...

SÓS: In the ashes.

In the ashes and in wretchedness as it were. And he was wasted away but he taught the Fianna a lesson. Anyway, he got up and walking with a feeble gait he caught the wether firmly by the ear without any difficulty and tied it up.

"Now," said he, "he'll stay put and you need have no fear."

They carried on and had the rest of the evening to themselves.

They ate and drank and thanked the young woman and were pleased with themselves. Then she said a few words:

"There isn't now a man among you of the Fianna who will not be granted a request – but just one request for each of you!"

SÓS: I see.

Very well then. She was down in the room and one by one each of them in turn went down to her. Well, Diarmaid Ó Duibhinn went down and she asked:

"What is your request?"

"That I be given a love spot," said Diarmaid, 'that I be given a love spot so that any young woman who saw it would fall in everlasting love with me."

Well he came back up... and every one of them, you know, was given his own gift. When Fionn went down to get his, she asked:

"What do you want, Fionn?"

"This much, oh stately maiden," said he, "that the smell of death be taken from me because I sinned with a dead woman."

SÓS: That was a strange request to make.

It was and it was granted to him. Yes. What was then that Oscar got? He got a thong. That may have been what he asked for – a thong that would last forever in his flail.

SÓS: Yes Indeed.

It is said that he is... He has plenty to do with his flail if he is still at the gates of hell with it. And he is busy there!

In the heel of the hunt, what Oisín asked for was God's grace. And the old saying has it since, that it was for this reason he went – was taken – to the Land of the Young and spent the time there until Christianity, until the priest was available to him. You know – that he stayed there all the time until St. Patrick was here to meet him.

SÓS: I see.

That's it.

SÓS: That was a great favour to get from God. Yes indeed. That's a lovely story, the young woman...

"Tether the sheep, Conán..." And there was another man to whom she said: "You had me before but you won't have me again."

SÓS: Yes. Then he asked the woman who she was.

Yes and what's that her name was?

SÓS: Youth.

Youth. She was youth.

SÓS: The woman was youth.

She was.

SÓS: He had her previously.

He had her previously.

SÓS: He would never have her again.

"You had me before," she said, "but you won't have me again."

The Legend of Slieve Mish/*Sliabh Mis*

The Slieve Mish mountain range lies at the eastern end of the Dingle Peninsula running for about 19 kilometers from Barnanageehy, towards Tralee, to *Cnoc na Stuaice* before it drops down to the sea at Inch on the southern coast. Half way across the range lies Caherconree, the site of the famous ancient fort of Cú Roí, and on the south-western side, towards Castlemaine, lies the site of a great battle between the Milesian invaders and the *Tuatha Dé Danann*. Some say the name is a confusion with Slemish mountain in County Antrim, with Mis being a female name, it means the mountain of Mis.

However, this explanation seems unlikely, as there is a legend of Mis, local to Kerry, a woman who lived in this mountain range and after whom it was named. This story of Mis is loosely based on a version of the myth that was first told to me by Eimear Burke from Kilkenny, many years ago.

*

Mis was the daughter of Dáire Dóidgheal (Dáire Mór), a powerful ruler from Europe who set out to invade Ireland. He landed with a huge army at Ventry beach, on the Dingle Peninsula, and a fierce battle ensued that is said to have lasted a year and a day. Dáire (sometimes referred to as King of the World) was eventually slain by the leader of the Fianna, Fionn mac Cumhaill, which brought the terrible battle to a swift end.

Mis, who was young and beautiful, came to the battlefield afterwards, in search of her father, and found only his dead body, covered in blood, on the beach. Mis was overwhelmed by grief on finding her father slain and threw herself down on his body, licking and sucking at his blood and wounds to try to heal him, much as an animal might do. Of course, her attempts to revive him were in vain and, what with all the blood and the horror of the situation, Mis became utterly mad and she ran screaming into the mountains, where she stayed alone for three hundred years (seven score years alternatively).

As time passed, stories grew of the untameable wild woman who lived in the mountains, and so the range became known as *Sliabh Mis*, such was her fame. In her grief, Mis forgot about the world below, she forgot that she was a woman, she even completely forgot that she was human and so she began to live the feral life of a creature of the wild.

Mis once had beautiful hair, but it soon became long trailing fur and feathers that covered her whole body. Her once tidy nails had become great razor-sharp claws, with which she attacked and killed animals and any person foolish enough to venture anywhere near her domain.

It was said that Mis could run like the wind, and no living thing was safe from her once she had a mind to catch it. The people of west Kerry thought her so dangerous that they created a no-mans-land, for fear of her - stripped of people and cattle, between themselves and the mountain range. And so it was that none but a fool would even think for a second of climbing up *Sliabh Mis*.

The king of Munster, Feidlimid mac Crimthainn, a devout ruler, offered a reward to anyone who was brave or daft enough to capture Mis alive. No-one accepted this challenge for years, fearing to lose their life, until one day, it was accepted by the gentle harper Dubh Ruis. People thought him mad when he made his way up into the mountains, unarmed and clutching only a sack of provisions and his smallest harp.

Dubh Ruis heard the screeching of Mis in the distance, but once he had reached a comfortable spot he calmly sat down to play his harp. Mis smelled the man from afar and ran in fury towards the smell, fully intending to kill and devour him. However, as she got closer she heard the beautiful tones of the harp and her murderous rage subsided, the strange music somehow reminding her of a far distant and faded memory.

Eventually, after a number of days, Dubh Ruis enticed Mis out of hiding and she found that she was able to speak to him and ask him - what was the sound that he made? He explained that it was music, and he continued to play to her, so that over the coming days, she began to remember some small fragments of human existence. One day, Mis saw Dubh Ruis standing by a rock to relieve himself, as men are prone to do, and she asked him what he had between his legs.

"That is my tricking stick!" he answered.

To which Mis asked "What else does it do?"

Dubh Ruis replied "Come and lie down here in the heather with me and I will show you!"

And so Dubh Ruis made love to Mis, much to their mutual enjoyment.

As time passed, what with the pleasures of the harp music and his 'tricking stick', Dubh Ruis coaxed Mis into a freshwater pool and, over several days, washed away the dirt and scrubbed away all of her feathers and fur. He combed her hair, so that it was beautiful and shining once more, and he fed her human food instead of the raw flesh that she had become accustomed to. He even made a bed for her and himself to lie on at night.

Eventually, long after he had been presumed dead, Dubh Ruis brought Mis back down the mountain and back to the world of men and women. He duly received a great reward from king Feidlimid mac Crimthainn, for this impressive feat. Not long after this, Dubh Ruis and Mis were married, living the rest of their days together in happiness as husband and wife.

The Last King of the Blaskets

Great Blasket (*An Blascaod Mór*) lies at the extreme west of Ireland, in the southwest at the end of the Dingle Peninsula. It has been unoccupied since November 17 1953, when the last remaining inhabitants of the Blasket Islands were permanently evacuated to the Irish mainland. Today Great Blasket is only occupied for the summer months, with basically only a caretaker living there for no more than the periods which tourists spend a day, a few days or weeks in visiting the island.

The Blasket Islands, are a group of six islands, consisting of Beginish, Inishabro, Inishvickillane, Inishtooskert, Tearaght and Great Blasket island, which is by far the largest. At its peak in 1916, Great Blasket had 176 Irish speaking people on it, but despite its tiny population it produced some important Irish language works such as *Twenty Years a-Growing*, by Maurice O'Sullivan, *The Islandman* by Tomas O'Crohan and of course Peig Sayers' *Peig - A Scéal Féin*. The whole island was Irish speaking, despite the establishment of a school in 1864, which encouraged the learning of the English language.

The evacuation was ordered by then *Taoiseach* Eamon de Valera, and it was largely regarded as a necessity, due to increasingly extreme weather patterns and the fact that the population by this time had dwindled to just 22 people. Up until 1929, the Blaskets had a "king" known as *An Rí* in *Gaeilge*. The last of these kings of the Blaskets was Pádraig Ó Catháin, who had died quite some time prior to the evacuation, in 1929 at the age of 73.

Pádraig was known as 'Peats Mhicí' to the Blasket islanders and like his grandfather, he was one of three "kings" over the last few hundred years of known history of the Blaskets. Pádraig Ó Guithín served as king during the early 1800s, with Pádraig Mhártain Ó Catháin (approx 1800-1900) serving during the mid 1800s, long before Pádraig Ó Catháin, who served from around 1900 onwards. These "reigns" were not continuous, with considerable decades between each one, perhaps because there was no particular need for a "king" during periods of relatively easy living or little need for leadership.

Of course, Great Blasket island, the only one of the islands that is truly habitable, has been occupied since the iron age, with remnants of beehive huts still in evidence today. It is possible they may well have had "kings" for a considerable part of its history. However, little is known of the history of the islands before the 1700s, with scarce mentions in historical records even then.

Perhaps with improvements in roads and the arrival of rail transport on the Dingle Peninsula, the population appears to have increased from the 18th century, rising to 140 in the mid 1800s, peaking at 176 in 1916, remaining fairly stable until its gradual decline from the 1920s onwards.

For a period of about twenty-five years, starting around the turn of the 20th century, Pádraig Ó Catháin served as "King of the Island" (*Rí an Oileán*), providing leadership to his small community of people, all of whom lived on the eastern side of the island, as the western half was suitable only for sheep and even they steered clear of it during the stormy months.

Impressive as it sounds, in fact, there was no official or legal power with the title of *An Rí* or "king", a suitable person was just chosen by the local community to serve the people, take responsibility in serious matters and perhaps be the final arbiter in community affairs. So Pádraig, it seems, had a position of responsibility and service rather than of power.

At this point in his life (around 1900-1904), Pádraig would have been in his forties, acting as the postman for the islands and he was also around ten years a widower. At this time, Pádraig was father to three sons and one daughter. He and his wife Eibhlín Ní Ghairbhia (who died in 1890) had six children in total but unfortunately the first, Seán, and their daughter Eibhlín died in their infancy.

It is recorded in *The Last King of the Blaskets* (by Gerald Hayes & Eliza Kane) that Pádraig had seven roles as "king". These were leader, postman, intermediary (newsreader), transporter (by boat), host-in-chief, advisor/counsellor and arbitrator. While most of these are fairly self-explanatory, the role of host-in-chief hails back to the ancient Gaelic culture of Ireland, when kings and chiefs were expected to provide generous hospitality to guests. In this role Pádraig would accommodate visitors to the island in his own house and act as a sort of ambassador/host.

As postman/transporter, Pádraig would make trips in his *naomhóg*, a type of *curach* (coracle), across Blasket Sound to the mainland at Dunquin (*Dún Chaoin*), generally twice a week. The *naomhóg* is descended from the ancient design of frame vessels that were covered with animal skins. The *naomhóg* was covered with waterproofed (tarred) canvas, but is basically a narrow and lightweight rowing boat that can be easily managed by one person, weather permitting. Such boats are still in use today, particularly by members of Dingle Rowing Club.

Of course, twice or even once a week was not possible much of the winter time, due to the frequent heavy seas and winter storms and on occasion Pádraig and other boatmen would have been trapped either on the island or the mainland, for weeks on end if they were particularly unlucky.

Being so incredibly isolated as they were, the islanders relied primarily on their "king" Pádraig Ó Catháin for news of the events on the mainland and indeed around the world. No doubt, as *An Rí*, Pádraig would have reported to the islanders the beginning of World War I in 1914, the Easter Rising of 1916, the Russian Bolshevik Revolution in 1917, the Spanish Flu pandemic of 1918, the end of WWI in 1918, the first non-stop transatlantic flight (ending in Ireland) in 1919, the Irish war of Independence 1919-1921, the Russian famine of 1921 and the Irish Civil War of 1922-23.

One can only wonder what such a small and insular community made of so many earth shattering events, both in Ireland and across the globe. It was certainly a time of great change and perhaps it is news of these monumental changes in society that led to the inevitable decline of island life on Great Blasket.

By the 1920s the youngest son Seán (known by the nickname *Seán An Rí*) helped his father with the post, now that he was in his later years, until Pádraig passed away in 1929. Seán continued as postman thereafter, but sadly he died some five years after his father, in 1934, and he had never been named as his successor, leaving his father Pádraig as the last "king"/ *An Rí*. In fact no successor was ever chosen between the death of Pádraig Ó Catháin in 1929 and the evacuation of the island in 1953. Perhaps as people had already begun the exodus to the Kerry mainland or further afield (such as England, Australia and America), it was no longer considered necessary.

Of the three other children who survived their father Pádraig, the eldest, Mícheál, had emigrated to America in 1902, Cáit moved to Dunquin in 1918, when she got married and Máire (who married in 1905) moved to Dunquin with the 1953 evacuation, where she lived until her death in 1970. A number of descendants of the last "king"/*An Rí* Pádraig Ó Catháin are still alive (at the time of writing) in both Ireland and America, proudly remembering the traditions of their 'royal' ancestor and the people of the now uninhabited Blasket Islands.

The Dingle Workhouse

The British New Poor Law, of 1834, sought to reverse the failure of the existing provisions for the poor in Britain by discouraging the provision of relief to anyone who refused to enter a workhouse. Many Poor Law authorities intended or succeeded in running workhouses at a profit, by utilising the free labour of their inmates. Most people were employed on tasks such as breaking stones, crushing bones to produce fertiliser, or picking oakum (tarred fibre used in shipbuilding especially).

Similar laws regarding workhouses were passed in Ireland four years later and the workhouse system in Ireland came into operation from 1840 onwards, created by the British government, as a means of providing food and shelter to the destitute. Similar institutions had existed in Britain itself since at least 1631, with origins dating back to 1388, but the system was woefully inadequate to cope with the level of destitution and starvation caused by the Great Famine that began in 1845.

The number of people seeking to go into the workhouses increased across Ireland, straining the system beyond breaking point – the workhouses were designed to hold a few hundred people at best, but were forced to cater for thousands. By March 1847, 130 workhouses across Ireland were filled to capacity with 115,000 people; by 1851 these same few buildings held an incredible 217,000 people in dire conditions.

In 1847 The Soup Kitchen Act was passed to provide food for people who could not get into the workhouses, despite the workhouses already being dangerously over-filled, there was still a huge demand and the vast numbers waiting to be let in could not be accommodated. The idea of the act was to provide some form of relief and sustenance to the homeless and starving, but just like previous legislation, it was woefully inadequate.

Dingle Workhouse was the last one to be built in Kerry, opening in 1850, ten years after the first Irish workhouse had been commissioned. It was intended to have accommodation for 700 inmates but by 1851 it had almost double that, with 1281 inmates, and a seemingly endless queue of those waiting for a place. Families were separated on entry to the workhouse, with quarters divided into male and female. Only male children under the age of two were allowed to remain with their mothers, otherwise they were taken away to the male quarters.

Under the provisions of the 1838 Poor Law Act, arrangements were such that the inmates should be "worse fed, worse clothed and worse lodged than the independent laborers of the district." As in Britain, the men had to break stones, or work on the land attached to the workhouse, while women in the workhouse were mending clothes, washing, or attending to the children and the sick. Death was very common in the Dingle Workhouse (as it was across Ireland) and burial grounds were opened nearby to facilitate burial of the steady flow of corpses. Kerry's population fell by 19% between 1841 and 1851, many of whom died while working in workhouses, such as the one built in Tralee.

An outbreak of cholera on the peninsula in 1834 thrust many into dire poverty, including those orphaned or left permanently disabled. The situation only got worse with the arrival of the potato famine in 1845. In 1847, often referred to as "Black 47", the Parish Warden of Dingle wrote to the Tralee Board of Guardians because Dingle temporary workhouses were so inferior that the desperate preferred to take their chances in Tralee. Already terrible conditions on the peninsula were exacerbated by a second cholera outbreak in Dingle in 1849. So, by the time that the government workhouse opened in 1850, there were already too many people looking to avail of it. Prior to this the starving and destitute were forced to walk up to 40 miles to Tralee to seek help, although most were turned away from the already overflowing workhouse there.

In the Dingle Parish Warden's letter of 1847 he stated:

"Since I received the resolution of the Board, there have been made to me over a hundred applications by parties seeking to be sent to the Workhouse in Tralee. They say they are satisfied to die after going there as they are sure of getting something to eat while life remains and of being buried in coffins."

In June 1846 Mr. Patrick Grey made an application at the County Special Sessions for the bulding of a Fever Hospital in Dingle, but the application was declined. The Tralee Board of Guardians passed a resolution in February 1848 that a building belonging to Patrick Grey and the old brewery belonging to Mr. Eager should be used as temporary workhouses. Over the next two years thirteen more temporary workhouses opened in the Dingle area – eleven of these were in the town with one twelve miles east at Liscarney and the last two miles west of Dingle at Monaree.

During this interim period (after 1846) a decision was made to build a permanent workhouse in Dingle and in January 1848,

Lord Ventry offered a free site (at the junction of Ashmount Terrace and Goat Street) for a workhouse and the Dingle Union was formed. By 1849 the potato famine itself had come to an end, although huge need remained. The workhouse and hospital building cost £6,850 with £1,380 for fittings.

The Report of the Poor Law Commissioners for Ireland in 1839 stated of workhouses that: "the style of the building is intended to be of the cheapest description compatible with durability; and effect is aimed at by harmony of proportion and simplicity of arrangement, all mere decoration being studiously excluded." Dingle Workhouse was no exception and was to be built to architect George Wilkinson's standard plan.

Despite the dire need in the area, it was not until August 1850 that a new building was erected and opened - Dingle Union Workhouse, Fever Hospital, School and Dispensary. Almost immediately it was overwhelmed far beyond its capacity, soon rising to nearly double the inmates it was designed for. At a time when Dingle was described as "one monster pauper asylum" the total number in the main and auxiliary workhouses was 4,848, which was 17.7% of the population of the peninsula. The ratio of workhouse inmates to general population in Dingle was 1:7, probably the worst in the country, and a good indication of the level of catastrophic starvation and disease. By comparison, the ratio was 1:14 in Skibbereen and 1:200 in Ballymena, Co. Antrim, yet Dingle was the last place in Kerry to gain a permanent workhouse.

Poverty continued to plague the peninsula long after the famine had officially ended. In 1889 four nuns came from the

St John's Convent of Mercy in Tralee to run the Dingle Union Workhouse and Hospital but by this time the Dingle Workhouse had just 189 inmates, of whom 69 were in the hospital. Even so, despite the low number of inmates, conditions were very poor, to say the least.

Before the arrival of the four nuns, the patients were on straw mattresses placed on raised planks and the bedclothes were, more often than not, soiled. The attendants at the workhouse were dirty and careless – food rations were thrown onto the beds as some patients weren't able to collect them for themselves. The windows were never washed and were thick with dust and grime and there were cobwebs everywhere.

Patients were so unkempt that it was said that they would frighten anyone who saw them. The Sisters recruited some respectable girls to help them, following their arrival at the pitiful and disgraceful workhouse, and with great patience and labour, conditions began to gradually improve.

In February 1922 the Board of Guardians was abolished and its functions were transferred to the Southern Health Board. Finally, Dingle Workhouse was closed that same year, seventy two years after it opened, and approximately 40 remaining inmates were transferred to Killarney. The building then became St Elizabeth's Hospital, which served the Dingle Peninsula until it closed in 2010, when the new West Kerry Community Hospital was opened. The building has been closed ever since, but still remains overlooking the town, empty until some use is found for it, or it eventually falls into ruin.

Inis Tuaisceart / Inishtooskert

To the west of Dunquin lies the island known today as The Dead Man or *An Fear Marbh*, as it has mostly been called on the Dingle Peninsula. It has several other names though - *Inis Tuaisceart* (Inishtooskert), which means the Northern Isle, presumably because it is the most northerly of the Blasket Islands, which is what the locals generally referred to it as. For some strange reason, it was also called *An tEaspag* (The Bishop) in the last century, but today it is most commonly referred to as "The Sleeping Giant", a somewhat more friendly name, which most tourists seem to know it as.

Viewed from the shore it does indeed look like a person lying down. Perhaps given the links with death and departure into the west of the souls of dead, that might explain the older and more macabre name. Like most of the islands near the coast of Dingle, there are signs of human habitation on the island, with a large number of ruined buildings, made of stone, that are of unknown age. Clearly, the island could not sustain human life for any long period of time, but presumably the ancient Irish came and went for some purpose that we do not know.

From the island you can clearly see Great Blasket to the south-east and "The Three Sisters" to the north-east. The Three Sisters (*An Triúr Deirfiúr*), are a group of three peaks on a section of land jutting out into the sea, known as Sybill Head, just north of the village of *Baile an Fheirtéaraigh*. The names of the three peaks are, from left to right, *Binn Hanraí, Binn Meánach* and *Binn Diarmada*, strangely none of which are female names.

Scarce few people get to see these sights from the island, as today the island of *An Fear Marbh* is a bird colony – full of important and rare seabirds, that prosper there, due to its remoteness and the total absence of human interference. In past times, White-Tailed Sea Eagles nested on a rocky pillar just off the northern coast, which appears from a distance to be part of the island.

A rocky outcrop, coming out of the sea by *Inis Tuaisceart* it is known to the Island people as *Cloch na Seasamh* (Upright Stone), which towers over the island itself. The occasional mainlander called it *Bod an Fhir Mhairbh* (The Dead Man's Penis), a somewhat cheeky name that would not go down well in the current social climate, but of course the islanders (not viewing from the mainland) knew it was not actually part of *Inis Tuaisceart*.

In his book *Dinnsheanchas na mBlascaoidai* (Place Names of the Blaskets), Tomás Ó Criomhthain mentioned that three men of the parish had climbed to the top of the pillar to the green patch on top (*Nead na bhFiolar*), where the eagles nested. Eagles' eggs could fetch £100 (punts) each, a lot of money in the early-mid 1800s, which the wealthy, especially in England, paid to have as ornaments.

Paddy an Oileáin, from Great Blasket claimed that Seán an Rí (son of the last 'King of the Blaskets') had climbed up *Cloch na Seasamh*. He was free-climbing without a rope, like his predecessors, and stole several eagle eggs, which he carried down in his cap, holding the cap in his mouth. Of course, with such a demand for eggs, the combination of greed and bravado of daring Blasket Island men soon obliterated the eagle population - with no more eggs the eagle colony died out. White-Tailed Sea Eagles have been extinct in Ireland for 100 years, until 10 were reintroduced to Killarney National Park in 2007. Their numbers are slowly beginning to rise, despite farmers' attempts to poison them, and maybe one day they might even return to *Cloch na Seasamh*. Today the eagles' eggs would be safe from egg stealers, as the Blasket Islanders are, like the White-Tailed Sea Eagle, extinct themselves.

The island of *Inis Tuaisceart* may now be unihabited by both eagles and humans, but it has been made famous around Kerry and beyond over the last 30 years, due to the children's book *The Sleeping Giant*, written by Irish author Marie-Louise Fitzpatrick. She is one of Ireland's most celebrated children's book authors and illustrators, having been awarded the prestigious Bisto/CBI Book of the Year Award on three occasions. *The Sleeping Giant*, which was Marie-Louise's second book, won a Bisto Award for Best Picture Book in 1992.

The re-introduced White-Tailed Sea Eagles of Kerry are protected and monitored by The Golden Eagle Trust. You can support their work at http://www.goldeneagle.ie

Gort An Ghalláin

Out in the townland of *An Ghráig* (Graigue) lies the café *Tig Áine*. It was opened some 47 years ago, by Áine Uí Dhúbhsláine with her husband Micheál, after having bought and rebuilt a ruined house from the late Mary Mhicí Ní Shúilleabháin. Mary was very fond of Micheál but not at all fond of Áine, so Áine says. However, knowing that they were looking to build a house, Mary sold them the ruined remains of her old house, from which stones had been taken to build a new house in 1935. She said "I'll sell you my old house, but a house is no good without a field, I'll give you *Gort an Ghalláin* as well."

Gort an Ghalláin (Field of the Menhir), is also known as *Gort na Sprice* - which means field of the projecting rock, but could also mean field of the boundary mark. Indeed the field, true to its name, contains a standing stone of almost 1.5m high, overlooking the sea, north of Clogher Head. The stone is of unknown age, its origin lost in the mists of time, but like many such stones - it has its own story.

And so, Micheál and Áine bought both the ruin and the field with the standing stone. They re-built the house and opened the first *Tig Áine*, in 1975, eventually moving it into the new building it is in today, in 2007. The one condition Mary had stipulated was that "Whatever you do, don't interfere with the standing stone! Because that's the place where the fairies of the two parishes meet."

It so happened that Micheál heard the very same story about the standing stone from another source, back in Dunquin

(*Dún Chaoin*). Of course, it is well known that it is best not to mess with the fairies, such as foolishly removing raths, standing stones or old hawthorns - to do so has often led to disastrous results for the reckless offender.

As Áine pointed out - in the local tradition, the stone was a kind of boundary, the meeting place for the fairies of the two parishes and some respect and care was required in regard to the stone and the fairies.

"From where I come in *Loch Gur*, my family going back a good bit, from the shores of *Loch Gur*, and there were lots of faires around there and in the history of the people. I would not like to upset the fairies, and I would call them *Na Daoine Maithe* (The Good People). That's what I would call the fairies."

"I think I am happy enough with our relationship with them. Just as the fairies are meeting out there, we are meeting in the café. We have weddings, funerals and baptisms and poetry reading and singing; particularly singing and dancing and people talking and eating and drinking. I think what we are doing there is supporting the fairies meeting in their meeting point, so that we are on different levels. I think it's a thing that worked out well."

The Piper and the New Shoes

A long time ago, there was once an uilleann piper who lived around the village of Lispole. One day, he walked into Dingle to buy himself a scythe and afterwards he decided to go to a pub before coming back home. By later that afternoon the piper was completely drunk and he began to stagger back homewards.

As he made his was way back, what did he see by the side of the road, only a dead man lying there. The dead man was wearing a delightful pair of new shoes, while the piper had only a raggedy and worn on out pair, torn half to bits. So, it was no wonder that the piper took an interest in the dead man's shoes and he had no fear of taking them, disrespectful to the dead as it was.

Now what did the piper do, but cut off the shoes. He had had some difficulty in removing the shoes as they were are a tight fit, or perhaps even the poor man's feet has swollen since his death. Having the brand new scythe with him, the piper cut off the feet of the dead man at the ankles and put them, shoes an all, under his armpit as a he carried on down the road, in search of some lodgings for the night.

After some time, he came to a farmhouse and the man of the house came out to him. Perhaps he didn't like the look of the piper, who had not yet fully sobered up at this stage, and he said to the piper "There is no room in the house, but you can sleep in the cowshed."

The piper duly carried himself off to the cowshed, where he slept until the morning. The piper arose early and after some great efforts took the new shoes, leaving the severed feet behind in the cowshed and he set off down the road again, towards his home in Lispole.

When the family in the farmhouse woke up, the farmer sent his son down to the cowshed to ask the piper in for some breakfast. When the son saw the shoeless feet lying there, he thought, not surprisingly, that the cow had eaten the piper during the night, and the feet was all that was left of him.

The boy ran back into the house and told everyone the story, and the family were very afraid. Later on, the farmer and his sons brought the feet away to be buried in the graveyard. The day after that, the farmer brought the poor 'guilty' cow down to Dingle Fair and it was sold. Afterwards, the family were on John Street, about to make their way home to Lispole, and they decided to go into a pub for a quick drink.

After they were served, they sat down to have their drinks, listening to the pleasant sounds of a jig. Who did they see in front of them but the very same piper, in his fancy new shoes, and he was up dancing like he was on fire!

Based an *as Gaeilge* traditional story in *Scéilín ó Bhéilín Scéalta Traidisiúnta don Aos Óg: Scéal ar Dhlúthdhiosca & Tionlacan Ceoil* by Roibeard Ó Cathasaigh (Editor) and Dómhnal Ó Bric (Illustrator), translated into English by Cyril Harrington.

The Wren Boys of Dingle

The Hunting of the Wren once included a wren being killed, attached to a pole and presented on doorsteps within the township/village by Wrenboys, singing a song and asking for money (or drink) to pay for the funeral of the bird. One of the feathers, which are thought to be lucky would be given to any contributing households, refusing to indulge them led to an angry rebuke and supposedly bad luck for the house.

In his 1922 epic tome *The Golden Bough*, Sir James George Frazer stated: "*A writer of the eighteenth century says that in Ireland the wren "is still hunted and killed by the peasants on Christmas Day, and on the following (St. Stephen's Day) he is carried about, hung by the leg, in the centre of two hoops, crossing each other at right angles, and a procession made in every village, of men, women, and children, singing an Irish catch, importing him to be the king of all birds." Down to the present time the "hunting of the wren" still takes place in parts of Leinster and Connaught. On Christmas Day or St. Stephen's Day the boys hunt and kill the wren, fasten it in the middle of a mass of holly and ivy on the top of a broomstick, and on St. Stephen's Day go about with it from house to house, singing:*

"The wren, the wren, the king of all birds,
St. Stephen's Day was caught in the furze;
Although he is little, his family's great,
I pray you, good landlady, give us a treat."

Traditionally in Ireland, the day after Christmas, St Stephen's Day was called Wren Day (*Lá an Dreoilín*) and the custom was once common, but the Wren has survived in Dingle. Today the event is a big attraction and draws a lot of tourists to the town, with car-loads of strangers, ready to join in the craic, arriving in often with costumes themselves.

There are four Wren groups in Dingle, all dressed in colours and straw hats and costumes - The Green and Gold Wren of O'Flaherty's Pub, *Sráid Eoin* Wren (John Street) in blue and white, The Quay Wren (Waterside) in green and white and lastly The Goat Street Wren in red and white. Good natured competition takes place, with mock battles between the teams. The Wrenboys also feature a hobby horse - a pantomime-type horse with a wooden head, snapping jaws and a cloth body stretched over a timber frame, which is worn on the shoulders of one of the members.

The origins of this bizarre custom go way back to the Pagan era, but have survived despite the condemnation of the Church, that referred to it as "an occasion of sin".

It usually gets going around midday, when the Wren groups make their way around the town, down towards the Marina and back up again, playing music as they go and these days, also raising money for charity. Traditional stops along the route include the Dingle Hospital, when each Wren visits the wards and bring some joyful festivities to the elderly patients.

After the parade is over, the music (and plenty of drinking) continues throughout the day and well into the evening for those with endurance, in the pub. However the modern version of the Wren is less rowdy than in earlier times, when drunken brawls were not unknown.

The Battle of Ventry (*Cath Finntrágha*)

Ventry Bay Beach (*Ceann/Fionn Trá*) is one of the most famous beaches on the Dingle Peninsula, not least because of this 12th century story that was translated into English by Kuno Meyer. It was published in 1885, from two velum 15th century codices, which were copied from earlier versions, now lost presumably.

The story centres around the invasion of Ireland by the King of the World (or King of the Great World), a title that appears in several Irish myths and also some Scottish myths. In this story the protagonist is Duire Donn, Dáire Dóidgheal or Dáire Mór, who is the father of Mis (associated with the *Sliabh Mis* mountains) who is resisted by Finn (Fionn mac Cumhaill) and the warriors of the *Fianna* warband, in a long and bloodthirsty battle (lasting a year and a day in some folklore). A new, beautifully illustrated, version of this classic story (*Cath Fionntrá*) was published in 2019 - written by Aogán Ó Muircheartaigh (in modern English and *Gaeilge*) and illustrated by Dómhnal Ó Bric (published by Dingle based publisher *An Sagart*).

The original English translation of *Cath Finntrága/Finntrágha* is presented here in full, along with the odd missing word or untranslatable (unknown) word, as edited by Kuno Meyer, 1885.

*

The Battle Of Ventry here below, i.e. the tragical death of Finn with the Fianna of Erinn, and the death of Duire Donn, the king of the great world.

A King assumed sovereignty and possession of the whole Great World entirely, namely Duire Donn (the Brown), the son of Losgenn Lomglunech (of the Bare Knees). Now, the hosts of the world gathered and assembled unto this King. There came Vulcan, the king of France, and Margaret, the Queen of Greece, and Fagartach, the king of India, and Lugman Lethanarmach (of the Broad Weapons), the king of the Saxons, and Fiachra Foltlebar (of the Long Hair), the king of the Gairian, and Tor the son of Breogan, the king of Spain, and Sligech the son of Sengarb, the king of the men of Cepda, and Herod the son of Dregan the son of Duille, the king of the men of Dregan, and Comur Cromgenn (of the Curved Sword), the king of the men of the Dogheads, and Caitchenn (the Cathead) the king of the men of the Catheads, and Caisel Clumach (of the Plumes), the king of Norway, and his three brothers, namely, Forne Glanger Gaiscedach (the Pure and Sharp and Valorous), and Mongach of the Sea, and Tacha, and Daire Dedsolus (of the Shining Teeth), the king of the Mediterranean, and Madan Muncas (of the Bent Neck), the son of Donn, the king of the Swamps, and three kings from the sunrise in the east, namely Dubcertan, the son of Firmas, and Muillenn, the son of Firlut, and Cuillenn the son of Faeburglas.

And now, when this weighty host had come where the high-King of the World was, they all fixed upon one plan, namely, to go and to take Erinn by fair means or foul. And this was the cause thereof. Once Finn the son of Cumall had been expelled from Erinn into the great world, and he was in the east during one year doing military service with Vulcan the king of France, and the wife and the daughter of the king of the Franks eloped with him, having both bestowed equal love upon him. And therefore those hosts and multitudes assembled to go and take revenge for it on the men of Erinn. For those brave ones did not think it honourable nor seemly that contempt and contumely should come upon them by a man of Erinn.

It was then the King of the World asked: 'Who is there that can be my guide in the harboursteads of Erinn?' he said. 'I shall guide thee true,' said Glas the son of Dreman. 'For I am myself expelled by Finn the son of Cumall, and I shall guide you about the smooth very broad harbours of Erinn,' said he.

Then came those numerous hosts and armies, and those proud henchmen to the harbour where their ships were, and their caravels; and their vessels and boats, their coracles and their beautiful ships were then made ready by them, and the trim straight oars with stiff shafts and hard blades were got out, and they made a strong eager quick powerful well-timed rowing so that the white-skinned foamy streams behind the ships from the quick rowing were like the white-plumed froth on blue rivers, or like the white chalk on high stones, so that... those ships over the billowy main and over the big great-crested slow blue waves.

Then arose the winds, and the waves grew high, so that they heard nothing but the furious mad sporting (unknown) of the mermaids, and the many crazy voices of the hovering terrified birds above the pure green waters that were in uproar. There was no welcome forsooth to him who got the service and the attendance of that angry, cold and deep sea, with the force of the waves and of the tide, and of the strong blasts consuming their... and their... and... against the vessels, nor was the babbling of those... pleasant, with the creaking of the ropes that were lashed into strings, and with the buffeting of the masts by the fierce winds that shivered them severely. There was not amongst them a vessel that was not shaken in its ribs, that was not... broken in its gear... in its board, shaken in its nails, rotten in its side, bruised in its... without water in its hold, ripped open in its..., shattered in its... overturned in its mast, severely bent in its stays, ...in its red canvas, lacerated in its boats, stopped in its swift career by the full gust of the storm, if the people of assistance and help near them had not come to aid it.

Now, when this storm did not find weakness on the heroes, nor debility on the champions, it rose from them, and went to its high lofty aerial abode. Then the sea grew gentle unto them, and every blue wave grew tame so that the ocean was mild, smooth, friendly in harbour and recess and corner and rock. And none of them had need to work or to row, but the slanting full-sailing ships went along with the sound of the pure-cold wind, until they took harbour and port on the goodly island of the worlds, and at the green rock that is called Scellig Michil to-day. It is he that was their guide there, namely, Glas the son of Dreman, from Sithan of Loch Lein of the cold water, and from the hidden places of Druim Droibel, and when a deer or other senseless beast was roused by the Fianna there was no need for a dog or a man to run after it, but it was caught alive by Glas the son of Dreman. And he was hired by the Fianna for that reason, and a short time he was with them when he was inveigled to betray Finn to Cormac the son of Art, the king of Erinn, and he had to leave Erinn for that, and to go into the great world, and it is he that was guide to the King of the World at that time.

'O soul, O Glas son of Dreman,' said the king of the world, 'not a harbour like this didst thou promise my fleet would find, but shores of white sand where my army might assemble for fairs and gatherings whenever they were not fighting.' 'I know a harbour like that in the west of Erinn,' said Glas, 'namely, Ventry Harbour in Corca Duibne (Corcaguiny).' They went onward thence to Ventry, and filled the borders of the whole harbour so that the sea was not visible between them, and the great barque of the king of the world was the first to take harbour, so that thenceforward its name was Rinn na Bairci (The Point of the Barque). And they let down their many-coloured linen-white sails, and raised their purple-mouthed speckled tents, and consumed their excellent savoury viands, and their fine intoxicating drinks, and their harps were brought to them for long playing, and their poets to sing their songs and their dark conceits to them.

'O Glas son of Dreman,' said the King of the World, 'to whom belongs this land into which we have come first as a portion of the spoil when they will divide Erinn between them before they return eastward?' 'To Tor the son of Breogan, the king of Spain,' said Glas, 'belongs this land.' 'In that case, O king of Spain,' said the King of the World, 'thou art obliged to procure entertainment and good cheer for us to-night.'

Then the king of Spain rose, and four red-armed battalions in order together with him, and he went at once across the border of the country, and there were three forts to the west of this territory, namely, Dun Cais, and Dun Aeda and Dun Cerbain, and they were burnt by the king of Spain, both kings and lords, both women and children, both dogs and men, both bowls and drinking-horns and cups, and there were thrice fifty henchmen in each of these forts, and they were all of them burnt by them.

Now Finn and the Fianna of Erinn knew that that heavy troop would come against Erinn, to wit, the kings of the whole world, as it had been represented and prophesied to them. And there was no landing-place in Erinn without a watchman from Finn over it, and he that was watching this harbour was Conncrithir the son of Bran, the son of Febal, from Temair Luachra. West from the Round Hill of the Fianna, that is called Cruachan Adrann, he was that night, and he asleep there; and what awoke him was the noise of the shields splitting, and the clashing of the swords, and the striking together of the spears cutting the bodies of the true warriors, and the cries of the women and children, of the dogs and horses in the flames. And Conncrithir arose at these cries, and what he said was: 'Great are the deeds that are done through my fault to-night,' he said, 'and woe to the mother that bore me, after the sleep I have made, and howbeit, Finn and the Fianna of Erinn shall not see me alive after this, and I will go into the midst of the foreigners so that some of them shall fall by me or till I fall by them.'

He girded his body in his battle-array and sent the swift-pointed .... of running after the foreigners. And not far did he go when he saw three women before him on the road, each of them dressed in a warrior's armour, and he ran after them, but did not overtake them, and he put his hand under his spear to throw it. 'Stop, O warrior,' said a woman of them, 'for thou knowest that it is not right for thee to redden thy arms on us (?), and we women.' 'Who are ye yourselves?' said Conncrithir. 'Three daughters of Terg the son of Dolar, from the shore of the sea Tiberias in the east are we,' said they, 'and we have all three fallen in love with thee from afar, and none of us loves thee less than the other; and we have come to help thee, for we knew that thou wouldst be the first man of the Fianna of Erinn that would make a stand against the foreigners.' 'What is your help to me to be?' said Conncrithir. 'Our help to thee will be good,' said they, 'for we shall form a druidical host around thee from the stalks of... and from the top of the watercress, and though armies and multitudes be killed around thee, they will cry to the foreigners, and beat their weapons out of their hands, and take away their strength and their sight. And the king of Spain and four hundred of his people will be killed by thee, and the battle of Ventry will be fought a day and a year, and there will be fresh fighting in it every day during that time. And be thou of good cheer, for even if thou art killed every day, thou wilt be whole again in the morning, for we shall have the well of healing for thee, and the warrior that thou lovest best of the Fianna of Erinn shall obtain the same as thou.'

Now the hosts of the king of Spain were taking plunder and materials (?) and silver from Traig Moduirn in the north, which is called Murbach at this time, to Ventry in the south. It was then that Conncrithir the son of Bran the son of Febal came upon them, and the druidical host with him, and he forced their plunder from them, and the druidical host took their strength and their sight from them, and the hosts of the king of Spain came in their rout and flight to the plain where the king of Spain was, and Conncrithir killing and destroying them.

'Stay with me, O kingly warrior,' said the king of Spain, 'that I may fight with thee for my people, since no man of them turns against thee, and thou slaughtering and slaying them.' So those two attacked one another, and they placed the two banners of soft silk into the green-sided earth, and stretched out the quick-wounding hands with the blue-headed red-socketed spears, and dealt black close hard insufferable wounds to each other, until the wounding rose high, and the shafts of their spears were broken, and they clove their shields, and they ripped open completely their hauberks, and they bared their purple-flaring broad-edged sword-blades, and prepared their deaths. And they were in this fight for a long time and while of the day, until Conncrithir struck a furious counter-blow (unknown) against the joint of the helmet and of the beautiful hauberk of the king of Spain, so that he smote his head off his body. And Conncrithir lifted up the head and boasted of the deed, and this is what he said: 'By my word, forsooth,' he said, 'I shall not let myself be separated from this head, unless I am killed, until some few or a great number of the Fianna of Erinn come to me.'

The King of the World heard that, and this is what he said: 'Great is that word which the warrior speaks,' said he, 'and rise thou and see who he is, O Glas son of Dreman, whether it is Oscar of the noble deeds whom I have heard of, of the Fianna of Erinn, that speaks this word.'

Then Glas went on shore and went near Conncrithir. 'O warrior,' said he, 'great is that word thou hast spoken, and what is thy name and thy family?' 'I am Conncrithir the son of Bran, the son of Febal, from Temair Luachra,' he said. 'If it is thou,' said Glas, 'thy blood and thy family are nearly related to me, for I am Glas the son of Dreman, from Temair Luachra,' he said. 'The less does it behove thee to come to fight against me from those foreigners,' said Conncrithir. 'It is sad,' said Glas, 'for the treasures of the whole world, if Finn and the Fianna of Erinn had been true to me, I should not fight against any man of Erinn nor against thee above all.' 'Do not say so,' said Conncrithir, 'for there are fifteen sons with Finn beside his own children, and I swear by my weapons and by my valour, that if thou hadst killed all these, thou wouldst not have to dread Finn, provided thou earnest under his honour and protection.' Thereupon Glas said: 'The day of fighting together with thee has come for me, and I will go and tell the King of the World.' And he went where the king was. 'O soul, O Glas,' said the king, 'is it Oscar that is there?' 'It is not he at all, O high king,' said Glas, 'and if it had been he that has come, it is not for thy people that he comes. It is an acquaintance and brother of mine that is there, and I am sick at heart that he is alone, and I desire to go and help him.' 'If thou goest,' said the King of the World, 'I demand of thee, to come and tell me the number that will fall by me of the Fianna of Erinn every day, and if some few of my host fall by them, to come and tell me by whom they shall fall.' 'I ask of thee,' said Glas, 'not to let any one of thy host ashore, but as I say, nor till the Fianna of Erinn come to us, and as there are no other restrictions for us to-day, let single combat be granted to us.'

And two foreigners were sent against them that day. And Conncrithir seized his long-sided sling, and put a straight even stone in it, and gave a straight well-directed cast, so that it went into the forehead of his adversary, and took the brain as a lump of blood out through the back of his head. So those two found their deaths by them, and they asked for two foreigners for either of them. This request was granted readily. Conncrithir lifted the thick spear of battle, and made a sharp quick determined (?) cast at the man next to him on their side, and hit him in the front of his breast, so that the spear went through him; and when the other man saw this, he fled behind the back of him that had been hit, so that the spear went through them both, and they found their death from it. And thereupon his own two fell through Glas. Three times nine fell through them before night, and Conncrithir was covered with wounds from that day, and he said to Glas: 'Three women have come to me from the shore of the sea of Tiberias in the east, and have promised me, though 1 should be killed every day in the battle of Ventry, I should be alive on the morrow, and that he whom I loved most of the Fianna of Erinn should obtain the same. And watch thou the harbour to-night, that I may go to seek them.' And he went to seek them, and they put him under the healing spring, and he came out whole.

As to Glas the son of Dreman, he went to the harbour. 'O king of the world,' said he, 'there is a friend of mine with the fleet, called Madan of the Bent Neck, the son of Donn, the king of the Swamps, and this is what he said in the great world in the east, that he himself would be sufficient for thee to take Erinn, and that he would bring it to do homage to thee by fair means or foul, and I ask thee to let him meet me alone tonight, that we may see which of us will better fight for Erinn.'

Then those two attacked each other and made a furious brave powerful fight, but as it was not in the destiny of Glas to find his death there, the king of the Swamps found his death by him. And shortly after that, Conncrithir came to him, and began to extol the deed which Glas had done, and to praise him highly. Then they saw a champion of the Fianna of Erinn coming towards them, to wit, the champion Taistellach. 'O youths,' said he, 'whose heads are those with you over the slaughter?' 'The head of the king of Spain is one of them,' said Conncrithir, 'and it is by me he has fallen. The head of the king of the Swamps is the other head, and by Glas the son of Dreman has he fallen. Hast thou got tidings of Finn and the Fianna of Erinn for us?' said they. 'I left them at Snam Da En in the north,' said Taistellach. 'Arise and seek them,' said they, 'and let them come to us, if they would preserve our lives.' 'That would be a shameful thing for me,' said the champion, 'that two kings of the Kings of the World should both have fallen by you, whilst my hands remain unreddened, before I go from the harbour.' And he went to the harbour. 'O King of the World,' said he, 'here is a champion of the Fianna of Erinn seeking fight.' 'It is I whom it behoves to answer that champion,' said Coimlethan the son of Toithem, to wit, the champion of the King of the World, and he came on shore forthwith.

Thus was this man, ten times twenty fists of a man in height and the same number in breadth, and moreover, he had bathed in the blood of dragons and lions and toads and venomous adders, and a broad girdle of strong leather was round his body. And the fierce heroes attacked each other in their firm-sided, rough-skinned, broad-footed, strong-tailed .... that were stout below, and let flash the great grey blunt eyes with their shaggy eyebrows, and they gnashed the grey-branched, strong-boned, chewing, wide-jawed board-like teeth, and they turned up the broad-caved, horrid, thin-branched, crooked noses, and those two warriors attacked each other, and closed the black and strong, never-sprained, firm-clenching, indissoluble hands across their backs, and gave each other mighty unequal (?) twists. Then the champion of the king of the world gave Taistellach a powerful right-valiant squeezing, so that he drew a drop of very red blood from the top of each of his fingers and a stream of dark blood over his lip, and he put him as a high wonderful load on his shoulder and carried him running to where the king of the world was, and Taistellach said: 'O soul, O Coimlethan, whatwouldst thou do to me?' 'To carry thee to the king of the world,' said he, 'and to tear thy head off thy body, and to put it on a stake in the presence of the men of the world.' 'That is a bad plan,' said Taistellach, 'for it is better for thee to let me down, that I may kneel before thee in the presence of the hosts of the world, and all the champions of Erinn have knelt before me, and will do so before thee, and moreover, it is pleasant for thee to be able to say in the great world in the east, that thou thyself didst sooner obtain the homage of the champions of Erinn than the

King of the World obtained their homage.' 'I pledge my faith,' said Coimlethan, 'that I will do so to thee,' and he let him down on the ground. Taistellach bent his head before him. He thought this was bowing to him. Taistellach stretched (his arms) around him and squeezed him mightily, angrily, strongly, till he reached the height of his shoulder, and the stone that was near him, he made a cast at him with it, so that he made bloody lumps of marrow of his body forsooth, to wit, of his skin, and he put his strong, broad-soled foot against his shoulder, and tore his head off his body, and boasted of his deed.

'May victory and blessing attend thee,' said Conncrithir, 'and go now to-night to the house of my father to Tcmair Luachra, namely, to Bran the son of Febal, and tell Bran to assemble all the *Tuatha Dé Danann* to help us, and thence betake thyself on the morrow to the Fianna of Erinn.' And Taistellach went his way after that combat to the fort of Bran the son of Febal, and related all his tidings to them completely.

Then Bran the son of Febal went to gather and muster the *Tuatha Dé Danann*, and he went to Dun Sesnain Sengabra in Conaill Gabra, and there was a feast being held there, and a great number of the youths of the *Tuatha Dé Danann* were there, and there were three noble sons of the *Tuatha Dé Danann*, namely, Ilbrech the son of Manannan, and Nemannach (the Pearly) the son of Oengus, and Sigmall the grandson of Midir, and they made Bran the son of Febal welcome, and desired him to stay. 'O youths,' said Bran, 'there is greater need than that for you,' and he began to tell them his story and to relate to them the strait that his son Conncrithir was in. 'Stay with me to-night,'said Sesnan, 'and my son Dolb the son of Sesnan will go to Bodb Derg (the Red), the son of the Dagda (the good god), and gather the *Tuatha Dé Danann* to us.'

And so they did, and Dolb the son of Sesnan went to Sid Ban Finn (the Sid of the White Women) above Mag Fernen, and there was Bodb Derg the son of the Dagda at that time, and Dolb related those stories to him. 'O youth,' said Bodb Derg, 'not we are bound to help the men of Erinn out of that strait.' 'Do not say so,' said Dolb, 'for there is not the son of a king or a prince or a leader of the Fianna of Erinn, whose wife, or whose mother or fostcrmother, or whose lemán is not from the *Tuatha Dé Danann*, and great help have they given you whenever you were in need.' 'We pledge our faith forsooth,' said Bodb Derg, 'that it is proper to respond to thee from the excellence of thy messengership,'and theysent off messengers to the Tiiathn DeDannnto where they were, and they came all to where Bodb Derg was, and they came to Dun Sesnain and stayed there that night, and they rose early on the morrow, and put on their costly silk shirts and their curling much-embroidered jubilee tunics, and their stout long-sided glittering coats of mail, and their ornamented helmets of gems and gold, and their sheltering green shields, and their heavy broad-sided strong swords, and their sharp-pointed tile-broad spears. And these were their kings and princes at that time, namely, the three Garbs of Sliab Mis, and the three Liaths of Luachra, and the three Muredachs of Maide, and the three Sichaires of the Suir, and the three Eochaids of Aine, and the three Loegaires of the Red Stones, and the three Conalls of Clomraige, and the three Finns of Findabair, and the three Seals of the Brug an Scail, and the three Rodanachs of Raigne, and the three Discertachs of Druim Fornachta, and the three sons of Aedan from Eas Ruaid mic Boduirn (the Salmon-Leap at Ballyshannon),andTathbuillech of Sliab Cairn, and Sochern of Mag Sainb, and the Segsa from Segáis, and Ferdron from Laigis (Leix), and the Glas from Bruinne Breg, and Airgetlam (Silver-hand) from the Shannon, and Ograide from Maenmag, and the Suirgech from Lemain, and the Sencha from the Shannon, and Midir from Brig Leith, and Feilim Nuacrothach, the son of Nochedal, and Donn from Sid Bec-Uisci (the Sid of the Little Water,) and Dregan Dronuallach (the Strong and Proud), and Fer an Berla Bhinn (the man of the Sweet Speech) from the Boyne, and Cathal Crithchosach (of the Trembling Feet) the king of Bernan Eile, and Donn Fritgrine, and Donn Duma, and Donn Teimech, and Donn Senchnuic, and Donn Chnuic an Dois, and Brat Riabhach (the Swarthy), and Dolb Dedsolus (the Bright-toothed) from the Sids, and the five sons of Finn from Sid Cairn Chain, and Finnbarr of Mega Siul, and Sigmall, the grandson of Midir, and Ilberach, the son of Manannan, and Nemannach, the son of Aengus, and Lir of Sid Finnachaid, and Abartach the son of Ildathach (the Many-coloured), and a great many other nobles of the *Tuatha Dé Danann* who are not enumerated here.

Now, these hosts and armies came into Ciarraige Luachra (Kerry) and to red-maned Slieve Mis, and thence to Ventry Harbour. 'O *Tuatha Dé Danann*,'said Abartach, 'let a high spirit and courage arise within you in the face of the battle of Ventry. For it will last for a day and a year, and the deed of every single man of you will be related to the end of the world, and fulfil now the big words ye have uttered in the drinking- houses.'

'Arise, O Glas, son of Dreman,' said Bodb Derg the son of the Dagda,'to announce combat for me to the king of the world.' Glas went where the king of the world was. 'O soul, O Glas,' said the king of the world, 'are those yonder the Fianna of Erinn?' 'Not they,' said Glas, 'but another lot of the men of Erinn, that dare not to be on the surface of the earth, but live in sid-brugs (fairy mansions) under the ground, called the *Tuatha Dé Danann*, and to announce battle from them have I come.' 'Who will answer the *Tuatha Dé Danann* for me?' said the king of the world. 'We will go against them,' said two of the kings of the world, namely, Comur Cromgenn, the king of the men of the Dogheads, and Caitchenn, the king of the men of the Catheads, and they had five red-armed battalions in order, and they went on shore forthwith in their great red waves.

'Who is there to match the king of the men of the Dogheads for me?' said Bodb Derg. 'I will go against him,'said Lir of Sid Finnachaid,'though I have heard that there is not in the great world a man of stronger arm than he.' 'Who of you will match the king of the men of the Catheads?' said Bodb Derg. 'I will match him,' said Abartach, the son of Ildathach, and he put on his heavy bright glittering coat of mail, and his crested, four-brimmed helmet of battle, and his sword...

Oscar of the great routs through the army of the foreigners, and like the wild, noisy, rough- streamed,terrible waterfall that pours through a narrow thin rock, or like a fierce red blaze of fire with high-peaked flames through the wide roof of a king's palace, or like the roar of a white-crested, green-skinned, wailing, white-foaming, full-watered wave of the great sea around it, so was the overthrowing and the scattering and the beating and the tearing into pieces and wild hacking which Oscar inflicted on the foreigners in that onslaught.

Then Vulcan the king of France and Oisin met each other, and they stuck their two banners of soft silk into the green-sided hill, and raised their two beautiful shields of many virtues against each other, and bared their terrible swords of smooth bronze, and made a ready, quick, successful onslaught. And the combat was going against one of them, for Oisin was being oppressed in it. And Oisin the son of Oisin saw this, and came towards them, and struck the king of France a blow, and the king returned the stroke and answered the ñghting of Oisin. And the two other sons of Oisin saw this, to wit, Echtach and Ulad, and they wounded the king of France, and he wounded either of them in exchange for his wound, and he elicited a sigh of oppression from Oisin over them all. And Mac Lugach saw this and wounded the king of France by a shot, and the king struck him a blow and answered the fighting of Oisin. Then came three times fifty warriors of the children of Baiscne to him, and every man of them wounded him, and he wounded every man of them, and he made Oisin utter a sigh of oppression over them all.

Now, this heard the pillar that was never put down, and the quickly-roused lion, and the venomous adder, and the wolf of combat, and the wave of overwhelming, and the (man of) destruction over the border, and the battle-gap of a hundred, and the hand which nobody dared to touch, and the heart that was never confounded, and the foot that never took one step backward before a few or many, to wit, Oscar of the noble deeds. And he was wondering who dared to bring his father into such a strait, and he came upon them in his angry, right terrible rush, and the terror that he struck into them was like (that of) fifty horses at a thunderstroke and at the shaking of the strand. And the king of France saw him coming towards himself, and his beauty and comeliness went from him, and his valour and his prowess left him, and he thought there was no shelter on earth for him, except if he went into the air or into the firmament, and he looked up into the clouds and thought that there was shelter for him between them. And there came lightness of mind and of nature upon him, and he gave his body a stretching from the ground, so that he went with the wind and with madness before the eyes of the hosts of the world, and did not stop in his mad flight till he came to Glenn Bolcain in the east of that territory. And wondrous great cries were raised by the hosts of the world in wailing him, and by the Fianna of Erinn in exultation.

Now, the Fianna of Erinn were thus till night came, and Finn said: 'Sad and sorrowful is the king of the world to-night,'said he, 'and he will make an attack of the harbour against you, and who is there of you that will take upon him the watch of the harbour to-night?' he said. 'I will,' said Oisin, 'with the same number that has been fighting together with me to-day, for it is not too much for us to fight for the Fianna of Erinn a day and a night.' And they went to the harbour. And that was the hour and the time that the king of the world said: 'It seems to us, O men of the world, our luck of battle was not good to-day,' said he, 'and let some of you arise to make an attack of the harbour on the Fianna of Erinn.'

Then arose the nine sons of Garb (the Fierce) the son of Tachar, namely, Donn Mara the son of Garb, and Lonnmar the son of Garb, and Lodra the son of Garb, and Iuchra the son of Garb, and Troiglethan (the Broad-footed) the son of Garb, and Tarraing Tren (the Strong) the son of Garb, and Tomna the son of Garb, and Dolar Durba the son of Garb, the king of the Sea of Wight. And sixteen hundred was their number, and they went all on shore except the eldest of those children of Garb, namely, Dolur Durba, and the children of Baiscne answered them readily and with fighting. And they began to beat each other severely, so that hands were hacked off there, and sides cut, and bodies mangled, and they continued in that fight until the morning came with its early light. And not one of them was alive on the morrow, that was able to wield his weapons on either side, but three of the children of Garb, and Oisin, and Oscar, and they did not let go of each other, but they made rushes at each other, and two of them attacked Oscar, and the third man and Oisin attacked each other, and hard, equally strong, and equally waged was that combat, and his own two found their death by Oscar, and the weakness and trance of death fell upon him, and that was enough to Oisin.

Then Oisin and the foreigner threw their weapons out of their hands, and closed their stout kingly graceful arms across the slender part of each other's bodies, and gave each other a manly right brave pull, so that it was worth coming from the east of the world to the lands of the men of the west to behold the fight of those two. Then the foreigner gave a sudden valiant pull to Oisin towards the sea. For he was a good swimmer and then Oisin gave him a pull, for he deemed it unmeet to refuse him his place of fighting. So they went into the sea together and were trying to drown each other, till they came upon the sand and gravel of the clear sea. Now, it was a heart's torment to the Fianna, that Oisin was in that strait. 'Arise, O Fergus Finnbel,' said Finn, 'to praise my son for me and to urge him on.' Fergus went to the harbour-stead of the white-shining foam. 'O soul, O Oisin,' said Fergus, 'good is the fight which thou doest, and many are those that witness it, for the hosts of the whole great world and the Fianna of Erinn are watching thee. And be thou courageous, and remember the good fights that have been accomplished by thee before this.' Then Oisin remembered his many great victories at the encouragement that he got from Fergus, and his courage rose high and his prowess grew great, and he closed the never-sprained fists about the slender part of the foreigner's back, and took him with him to the sand of the clear sea, and put his back to the sand and his face upward, and did not allow him to get up, until his soul had departed from his body. And he took him on shore and severed his head from his body, and came himself to the Fianna of Erinn triumphantly, vauntingly.

Then arose the eldest of those children of Garb the son of Tachar, namely Dolar Durba, the king of the Sea of Wight. 'O king of the world,' said he, 'it was a sad thing for thee, not to have let me together with my brothers against the Fianna of Erinn, for if I had been with them, the Fianna of Erinn would not have been able to kill us, and I will avenge them well, for I will kill one hundred armed men of them every day until I have done with them all, and I pledge my word,' said he, 'that if I find any of the hosts of the world reddening their weapons on any of them, I shall put him to death.' And he went on shore, and challenged one hundred of the Fianna to fight, and there was uttered by them a shout of contempt and derision at him, and one hundred were put against him on that day. However, his attack on them was the rush of a fierce barbarous lion, and they fell by him without his receiving a wound or getting bloody, and he made a cairn of their heads, and a mound of their trunks, and a cairn of byrnies of their accoutrements.

Thereupon the foreigner doffed his battle-dress, and donned a splendid elegant dress, and took a club and a ball, and beat the ball from the west of the strand to the east, and he caught it in his right hand before it descended, and he put it on his foot the second time, and he sprang in his rushing from the west of the strand to the east, and he threw the ball from one foot on to the other, without touching it with the hand, and without its touching the ground, and he put it on his knee the third time, and ran to the other end of the strand, and then put it from one knee on to the other, without throwing it on the ground. Then he threw it on his shoulder and made a rush like the March wind from one end of the strand to the other, and then sent the ball from one shoulder to the other, without touching it with the hand, and without throwing it on the ground, and he challenged all the Fianna to perform that trick. Now Oscar and Mac Lugach were ready to go and to perform that trick. 'Stay,

O youths,' said Finn, 'for no man of Erinn ever performed or will perform that trick but three only, namely Lug the son of Eithle in the battle of Mag Tured (Moytura), and Cuchulaind performed it at Tailltin (Teltown), and there will come another youth from Connaught who will perform it.'

After that the foreigner went into his ship, and he came on the morrow and sought the conflict of a hundred. There was not found anybody to accept it, so that the Fianna cast lots, and of the hundred that went against him on that day, there escaped not a man of them to tell the tidings, and they fell by him forthwith. And he went into his ship for that night. He came to them on the morrow, and never did the Fianna let a man challenge them to fight for a longer time without answering, than him, and it was a hard thing for them to cast lots when no answer had come forth. And the hundred who had to go against him on that day, did leave wishes for life and health with the Fianna of Erinn, for they knew that they would not come back again. The foreigner came towards them, and such was his fury, that he took no weapons with him on that day, but he made a rush through them, and the man that was next to him, he seized at the slender part of his foot, and aimed a mighty shot with him at the head of the next man. And those hundred fell by him, and he let forth his warrior's voice from the top of his head, boasting of the slaughter. And he went into his ship for that night.

Now, the story of this foreigner and the destruction he had brought on the Fianna was heard throughout the four corners of Erinn. Then Fiachra Foltlebar (of the Long Hair), the king of Ulster, heard this and said: 'I am sad,' said he, 'on account of the greatness of the calamity in which the men of Erinn are, and that I am not myself able to fight along with them.' And he had no issue but one son only, thirteen years old, and he was a prince the fairest of figure and face that was in Erinn. 'Well mightest thou do this,' said the boy, 'namely, to send all the youths of Ulster with me to them, as thou art not able to fight thyself.' 'Do not say so,' said the king, 'for a child of thirteen years is not fit for fighting, and if such a one were, thou wouldst be so.' And the king perceived that the boy did not wish to live without going to the Fianna of Erinn. Therefore he was seized by them and put into a chamber under lock, and twelve sons of the kings and chieftains of Ulster that were his foster-brothers together with him. 'O youths,' said the boy, 'you would do well, if you went with me to the Fianna of Erinn; for though your fame goes along with the kingship of Ulster, it would be good for you, if you had a good name of your own. For though Conall Cernach the son of Amargin, or Cuchulaind the son of Sualtam, or the noble prosperous sons of Usnech have not possessed the kingship of Ulster, yet Conchobur with whom was the kingship of Ulster was scarcely more illustrious than they through their own brave deeds, and I pledge my word moreover,' said he, 'that food or eating shall not pass over my lips ever for the wrongs (done) to you, so that I shall find death, and a foreign king will take the kingship of Ulster after my father and pass wrong judgments upon you.'

Now, this speech went round among the youths, and when the king was asleep, they went into the armoury, and every boy took a shield, and a sword, and a helmet, and two battle-spears, and two whelps of a greyhound out with him. And they went across Ess Ruaid mic Baduirn in the north, and straight through the fertile lands of Cairbre, and through the province of Connaught of numerous clans, and through Caille an Chosnuma (the Woods of Defence) which are called Roga Cacha Rigi and Fironoir Cacha Filed (Choice of every Kingship and True Honour of every Poet), and across the river Anaige, and into Kerry, and by Cathair na Claenrath (the Town of the Sloping Forts) in the west, and thence to Ventry Harbour.

That was the hour and time, that the foreigner, namely Dolar Durba, came upon the strand to incite and to revile the Fianna, and great shame seized Oisin on account of this. 'Ye Fianna of Erinn,' said he, 'a great number of our men have fallen by Dolar Durba, and I do not think that many of us will return alive from the battle of Ventry, and if it is my fate to find death in it, I will rather find it through Dolar Durba, and fight a brave combat against him, than witness the destruction he will bring upon the Fianna every day.' And a sad woeful heavy passionate cry was raised by the warriors of the Fianna, and by their minstrels, and gleemen, and wise men, at those words of Oisin.

That was the hour and the time, that they saw the young varied troop coming straight towards them from the east to the harbour. 'Stay with me, O son,' said Finn, 'that I may know whose is this young varied troop which I behold, the fairest of appearance that I have ever seen in the world.' And thereupon they approached them, and the son of the king of Ulster let down his right knee before the king of the Fianna, and greeted him modestly and sensibly. And he was answered in the same way, and Finn asked tidings of him who they were and where their home was. 'Emain Macha is our home,' said the boy, 'and I myself am called Goll the son of the king of Ulster, and those other youths whom ye see are my foster-brothers.' 'What have ye set out for at this time?' said Finn. 'We heard that the army of the whole great world was fighting against you every day, and we were desirous to learn feats of valour and bravery from you, and if there were young noble boys like us accompanying the king of the world, we should like, O king of the Fianna, to ward off from thee an equal number of them, as we are not of a proper age for the combat of choice heroes.' 'Welcome is your coming and your arrival,' said Finn. 'Howbeit, it would be a great thing to let the only son of thy father go against the foreigners, there being no royal heir for the men of Ulster but he.'

Just then the foreigner let forth his warrior's voice at the top of his head to defy the Fianna. 'What is yon warrior that I see,' said the son of the king of Ulster. 'That is a warrior challenging one hundred to fight,' said Conan the son of Morna. 'What causes it that he does not obtain single combat?' said the boy. 'That is a sad thing,' said Conan, 'for five hundred warriors of the Fianna have fallen by him during five days one after the other, and now there are not found a few or many to answer his challenge.' 'Wonderful is the fame that is on you,' said the youth, 'whilst a single warrior in the world is refused combat by you. And I will encounter him,' said the son of the king of Ulster. 'Do not say that again,' said Conan, 'for, by our word, the five hundred that fell by him, every one of them would be a match for thee.' 'I did not know the Fianna till now,' said the youth,' and I think that thou, O son of Morna, art the man of bad manners and bad language among the Fianna.' 'It is of me that is said,' said Conan. 'I pledge my word,' said the son of the king of Ulster, 'that if thou and yon warrior and those five hundred were on one side, I should not move back one step before you all.' And the boy rose to meet the foreigner.

'Ye children of Ronan,' said Finn, 'I charge you by your pledge and honour, not to let the son of the king of Ulster go against the foreigner.' Cailte and all the children of Roñan arose, and it was heavy work for them all to bind him, and fetters and bonds were put on him. And while they were holding him, his twelve foster-brothers went to fight with the foreigner, and the Fianna did not notice them, till they had fallen by him, and till he had struck off their twelve heads. And he sent forth his warrior's voice at the top of his head, boasting of that deed. 'What does the foreigner do this for?' said the son of the king of Ulster. 'Sad for thee is the reason,' said Conan the son of Morna, 'for he is boasting of thy twelve foster-brothers.' 'Sad is that story, O man,' said the son of the king of Ulster, 'and O ye Fianna of Erinn, long will be the blame for this on you, to keep me like this, for I shall die of anger and shame, and it is upon you that the blame will be,' said he, 'and ye and the men of Ulster will be foes after this for ever, and small would have been the loss for you, if I had fallen by yon foreigner, before ye bound me like this."

Now, this speech went round among the Fianna of Erinn, and he was loosened by them on account of it. Then that boy took the weapons of his elders and of his seniors, and put on a shirt of silk and a great grey long blue coat of mail, and a golden shield with purple borders, and an ornamented slender-wrinkled white-edged collar, and two blue-pointed broad-headed stout-socketed spears, and an ornamented sword with a golden cross-hilt. And he made a rush against the foreigner in that wise. And the foreigner smiled when he saw him approaching, and the whole army of the great world raised cries of derision and jeering at him, and the courage of the boy was all the greater, and he inflicted six wounds on the foreigner, before he was wounded himself. And they fought a combat sharp, bloody, masterly (?), evenly matched, valiant, courageous, powerful, proud, murderous, dashing, red-sided, sudden-wounding, terrible, wonderful, unheard-of, howling, quick, groanful, red-handed, brave, quick-wounding, eager, close, mad, furious, wound-giving, red-speared, courageous was the combat of those two. For if search were made from the eastern borders of the island of Cirbam, to wit, of the Red Sea to the land of the western people, there would not be found between them a braver combat of two than that combat. And the hosts of the whole great world and the fíanns of Erinn were urging them on.

And when now the night had come, and when their weapons were broken, and their shields split, they did not leave off from each other, as it is customary to put off combat if night should come on, but they made a strong angry awful rush at each other, and closed their nimble strong hands across each other, and gave each other quick dexterous pulls, so that they made the white sandy shore seethe. And they continued in that embrace, until the tide of the sea came and spread between them and the land, and such was the fury of those two, that they did not give up their place of combat, till the tide of the sea came over them, so that they were both drowned before the eyes of the hosts of the world and of the Fianna of Erinn. And an exceeding great cry was raised by the hosts of the world and the Fianna of Erinn, bewailing those two. And it is there they were found on the morrow upon the beach, and their hands locked hard across one another's graceful backs, and their feet were tightly locked through each other, and the nose of the son of the king of Ulster was in the mouth of the foreigner, and his chin was in the mouth of the youth, and it was necessary to cut the foreigner in disentangling them. And the son of the king of Ulster was buried, and his grave was dug, and a flagstone was raised over his tomb, and his funeral games were held by the Fianna of Erinn. And never before there fell through a hero's weapons a youth for whom the sorrow was more general than for him.

'Who will keep the watch of the harbour to-night?' said Finn. 'We will go thither,' said the nine Garbs of the Fianna, to wit, Garb of Slieve Mis, and Garb of Slieve Cua, and Garb of Slieve Glair, and Garb of Slieve Crot, and Garb of Slieve Muicce, and Garb of Slieve Fuait, and Garb of Slieve Atha Moir and Garb of Dundalk, and Garb of Dun Sobairchi, and their own Fianna together with them. They were there but a short time, when they saw Herod the son of Dregan, the son of Duille, the king of the men of Dregan, coming towards them, and they attacked each other, and were slaughtering and destroying each other. But it is impossible to relate and to describe their whole combat, nor can one give their description, for at the end of the day there were not standing of them, but three

Garbs, and the king of the men of Dregan. And not weakness nor fear did the greatness of the slaughter round about them cause them, but they bent their heads, and nimbly moved their hands, and every one of them lost the sense out of his soul, for they thrust the spears into the bodies, so that they took out clotted particles of red-frothing blood through the backs of the good heroes. And those four fell together, sole against sole, and lip against lip, on that battlefield.

Thereafter Fergus Finnbel (of the Fair Lips) the son of Finn beheld the great number of the Fianna of Erinn that had fallen, and he went without leave, without counsel of them to Temair na Rig (Tara of the Kings), where Cormac the son of Art, the high king of Erinn, was, and he told him of the strait in which Finn and the Fianna of Erinn were. 'I am pleased,' said Cormac, 'that Finn is in that strait, for not one of the husbandmen that we (shall) have dares to touch a pig, or an animal, or a trout, or salmon, or a roebuck, when he finds it dead at the head of any road, he dares not to take it up from the ground on account of the charge, and no husbandman dares to go from his country place to the old town without paying a screpal to Finn, and none of their women dares be given to a man until she be asked, whether she has a man or a lemán of the Fianna of Erinn, and if she has none, a screpal must be paid to Finn before she may marry. And many are the wrong judgments that Finn has passed on us, and for us victory with the foreigners would be better than with him.'

Then Fergus went on the green where Cairbre Lifechair the son of Cormac was at a game of loop and ball. 'O Cairbre

Lifechair,' said Fergus Finnbel, 'badly art thou defending Erinn in playing an idle game without lasting gain, while she (Erinn) is being taken from you by foreigners.' And he kept urging him on and rebuking him, and great shame seized Cairbre Lifechair on account of this, and he threw his club from him, and went among the people of Tara, and brought together all the youths, so that they were one thousand and twenty on the place. And they march off without leave, without counsel from Comrac the son of Art, until they reached Ventry Harbour. And Fergus went before them into the tent of Finn, and Finn asked tidings of him, and Fergus told him that Cairbre Lifechair had come with him. And all the Fianna of Erinn rose before Cairbre, and bade him welcome. Said Finn: 'O Cairbre,' said he, 'we should have liked thy coming to us better at a time when minstrels and gleemen and poets and ladies and gentlewomen might have made thee merry, than when the need of battle is upon us as it is now.' 'Not to attend thee have I come," said Cairbre, 'but to offer thee my service in battle.' 'I have never taken an inexperienced youth to the bosom of battle,' said Finn, 'for it often happens that he who comes like that, goes where he finds his death, and I do not wish that an inexperienced youth should fall through me.' 'I pledge my faith,' said Cairbri, 'that I will give them battle on my own account, if thou doest not do it on thine.' And Fergus Finnbel went to announce combat from Cairbre Lifechair to the king of the world.

'Who will answer the son of the king of Erinn for me?' said the King of the World. 'I will go against him,' said Sligech the son of Sengarb, the king of the men of Cepda, and he went on shore, and his three great red battalions. And Cairbre encountered them, and all the youths that accompanied them (unknown) were near Cairbre there. 'O Cairbre,' said a man of his people to him, 'take to thee a bold heart for this fight; for the Fianna will not be better pleased with thy good luck in it than with that of the foreigners. For it is thy grandfather that killed Cumall the son of Trenmor, the father of Finn, and they do remember that, though thou doest not remember it.' When Cairbre heard that, he made a rush through the battalion of the foreigners, and began slaying them and prostrating them, so that the sides of the strong warriors were cut by his onslaught, and the nobles were destroyed by his great fight. Then an angry destructive man met him, to wit, Sligech the son of Sengarb, and though it was ready death and sudden destruction and certain ruin to meet him in combat, they both struck out at each other, and they took hold of their two beautiful shields of many victories, and they bent down their high renowned countenances from the borders of the variegated and lofty shields with the elegant rims, and they wielded the burnished blades, so that the sides were holed, hewn hurdles, cut open from that powerful conflict... with these weapons to Finn towards the hour of battle to-day.'

Then Mac Eimin went his way with the swiftness of a swallow or a hare (?) or a fawn, or like the gusts of a pure-cold wind coming over the top of a plain or of a field-road, until, at the hour of rising in the day, he reached Ventry Harbour. That was the hour and the time that Fergus Finnbel was urging on the Fianna towards the great fight, and this is what he said: 'Ye Fianna of Erinn,' he said, 'if there were seven equal days in one day, here is their work for you to-day; for there never was, or ever will be done in Erinn work of one day like (the work of) to-day.'

Then the Fianna of Erinn arose, and as they were there, they beheld Mac Eimin in his rush of quick running coming towards them, and Finn asked tidings of him, and asked him whence he did come. 'From the brug of Tadg the son of Nuadu have I come,' said Mac Eimin, 'and to thee have I been sent, to ask thee, how it comes that ye go against the King of the World and do not redden your arms or many weapons upon him.' 'I pledge my faith,' said Finn, 'that if my weapons do not get reddened on him, his body shall be crushed by me in the midst of his coat of mail.' 'O king of the Fianna,' said Mac Eimin, 'I have here with me the venomous weapons through which he is fated to find death, and Labraid Lamfhada (L. of the Long Hand), the brother of thy own mother, has sent them to thee through druidical sorcery.' And he placed them into the hand of Finn, and he took their coverings off them, and there arose from them fiery flashes of lightning, and most venomous bubbles, and the warriors could not endure looking at those weapons, and one third of prowess and valour and courage and high spirits came into every man of the Fianna of Erinn as he beheld those weapons with Finn. For the balls of fire they sent forth, no dress or garment could resist them, but they went through the bodies of the men next to them like most venomous arrows. And Finn said: 'Go, O Fergus Finnbel,' said he, 'and see how many of the Fianna remain for the great fight to-day.' Then Fergus Finnbel counted them, and said to Finn: 'One battalion in order alone remains of the Fianna,' said he, 'and many are the men in it, that are able to fight three, and those that are able to fight nine, and thirty, and a hundred.' 'Arise, if it be so,' said Finn, 'to where the King of the World is, and tell him to betake himself forthwith to the place of the great fight.'

Fergus went to the King of the World, and the king was just on his couch, and music of harps and of flutes was being played to him. 'O King of the World,' said Fergus Finnbel, 'long is that sleep in which thou art, and no shame for thee, for this will be thy last sleep. And the Fianna have gone to their places of fight, and do thou answer them.' 'It seems to me,' said the King of the World, 'there cannot be a youth of them capable of fighting against me, and how many remain of the Fianna of Erinn?' he said. 'One battalion in order only,' said Fergus, 'and how many of the hosts of the world do remain?' 'With thirty battalions have I come to Erinn,'said he,'and twenty battalions of them have fallen by the Fianna of Erinn, and this is what remains of them, ten red-weaponed battalions in order. And howbeit, there are eight of them, and if the men of the whole world were against me, they would be overcome by them, to wit, (by) myself and Conmael, my son of great deeds, and Ogarmach, the daughter of the king of Greece, the best hand in the world after myself, and Finnachta Fiaclach (of the Teeth), the leader of my henchmen, and the king of Norway, and his three brothers, to wit, Caisel Clumach and Forne danger Gaiscedach, and Tocha, and Mongach of the sea.'

'I pledge my word, forsooth,' said the king of Norway with his brothers, 'if any man of the hosts of the world go against them before us, we shall not go, for it would not be an occasion of reddening our weapons on them, and we should not give them our old (accustomed) satisfaction, for it is a thing forbidden to us to redden our weapons unless they get their fill of blood and of gore.'

'I will encounter them alone,' said the youngest of that family, to wit, Forne the son of the king of Norway, and he put on his grey-venomous frightful blue dress, and he went among the Fianna of Erinn, with a red-edged sword in either hand, and he dealt destructive blows in turn among them, and he destroyed what was sent against him of their youths. And he made the strand narrow with their champions, and he filled the plain with their warriors. And Finn saw this, and the destruction that the foreigner dealt among the Fianna was torment of heart, and danger of death, and loss of mind to him, and he kept urging the Fianna on against him, and Fergus Finnbel arose, and this is what he said: 'Ye Fianna of Erinn,' said he, 'it is a sad thing that ye have got into such a strait and oppression which ye have suffered in defending Erinn, and one warrior taking her from you to-day, and not otherwise are ye but like flocks of small birds in some bush seeking shelter when a hawk is pursuing them, so are ye going into the shelter of Finn and Oisin and Oscar, and none of you is better than the other, and none of you gives his face against the foreigner.' 'By my faith,' said Oisin, 'all that speech is true, and none of us tries to excel the other in warding him off.' 'There is none of you that is better than the other,' said Fergus. 'Do now,' said Oisin, 'let forth a vehement thundering noise against the foreigner. Stay with me, O warrior,' said Oisin, 'that I may fight with thee for the Fianna.' 'I pledge my word that this respite will be short,' said the son of the king of Norway.

Then they raised their two beautifully-bordered shields with speckled points against each other, and poised the frightfully-wounding fearful spears, and the iron-bladed gold- ornamented swords, and made a quick vehement attack for a long time. Now, the combat was going against one of them there, for Oisin was being overthrown, and he sent forth a sigh of unequal combat; and it was back towards life, and bereavement of intention of help to the Fianna, that Oisin was in that strait. And a woeful cry was raised aloud for him.

'I pledge my word, O man of poetry,' said Finn to Fergus, 'that the urging thou hast given to my son against the foreigner was sorry. For I would rather that I myself and all the Fianna of Erinn should find death, than that I should behold him in the strait in which he is. And rise thou to praise my son for me, so that his courage may be the higher, and his fighting the more valiant.'

Fergus went to the place where the heroes were fighting. 'O soul, O Oisin,' said Fergus, 'the Fianna are greatly ashamed of the lowness of thy place in this combat, and there is many a foot-messenger and horseman... from daughters of kings and princes of Erinn watching thy fighting.' A high spirit came over Oisin at that incitement which Fergus gave him, and his courage rose, and his spirit grew high at his praising, and he gave a stretching to his body, so that a child of one month would find room between every two ribs of his, and all the Fianna heard the creaking of his bones being pressed from each other, and he made a cast with his red-socketed battle-spear that he had, so that the spear went into the breast of the hauberk, and the length of a man's hand of the hard four-edged shaft followed the blue iron through his back out behind, so that he found death of it. And he himself came back to the Fianna of Erinn.

Then an enormous great cry was raised by the hosts of the world wailing him, and another cry by the Fianna of Erinn extolling him. But the loss of this hero did not cause weakness or fear with his brothers, for they deemed it not good or seemly that he should have fallen by a warrior of the Fianna. Then arose the fierce impetuous true warrior that was called Tocha, the son of the king of Norway, and he went on shore to avenge his brother. And thus was that man: a round of iron boards like a shower of venom about him from his sole to his crown. It was change of countenance for a man to look at him even though he did not attack him, and the face of brave soldiers grew black, and true warriors lost their power, and heroes lost their mind in looking at him. And he staid not in their flank, but went right into the midst of the Fianna, and gave his burnished elegant blade a feeding on the bodies of heroes, and on the shoulders of true warriors, and on the shoulders of champions, and on the breasts of kingly soldiers, and they all turned their back to the foreigner, and went in the rush of rout and flight before him. Now, though that strait was a great shame, yet nobody took it upon him to ward off the son of the king of Norway, until Mac Lugach turned round against him.

'Stay with me, O kingly soldier,' said Mac Lugach, 'that I may fight with thee for the Fianna, since they all do not undertake to meet thee.' Now it was with the son of the king of Norway, to turn from the red slaughter in which he was engaged, and though it was, he did not deem it seemly that his honour should be to wit, to refuse combat to any body.

Then those two fought a terrible many-wounding unheard-of high combat without interruption, without quarter, without a thought of weakness, or fear, or flight on either of them, so that their spears crumbled in the fight, and the blades bent with their continual striking, and their shields were shattered by the edges of the sharp-pointed heroes' swords, and they lost their golden shields. It was then the great combat grew keen, and they gave at the same time two proud terrible quick successful counterstrokes, so that the swords struck each other in their thin edges, in such wise that the sword of Mac Lugach went through the sword of the foreigner, and he gave another stroke to him, so that he broke the helmet, and quickly clove the firm hauberk, and split the shield, and cut the heart equally in two by that subtle stroke. And he came himself proudly high-spiritedly to the Fianna of Erinn.

Then arose the other foolish inconsiderate courageous son of the sons of the king of Lochlann, whose name was Mongach of the sea, and all the hosts of the world rose together with him. 'Stay, ye men of the world,' said he, 'for it is not ye have to demand body-eric for my brothers, and as it is not ye, I must myself go and demand the first eric from the Fianna of Erinn.' And he went on shore. And it is thus he was, with a strong iron flail in his hand, with seven balls of refined iron, and fifty iron chains from it, and fifty apples on each chain, and fifty venomous thorns on each apple. And he made a rush through them in that shape to utterly smash them, and to tear them into strings, and to destroy them, so that the dispersing and flight he caused among the Fianna round about him was like (that of) a flock of small birds fleeing before a hawk. And great shame seized upon a warrior of the Fianna of Erinn on account of this, to wit, Fidach, the son of the king of the Bretons, and he said: 'Come and praise me, O Fergus Finnbel,' said he, 'that I may go and fight the foreigner, and that my courage and my spirits may be greater and my fighting braver when thou art praising me.' 'Easy is it to praise thee, O son,' said Fergus, and he kept praising him for a long time.

Then those two contemplated each other with their looks, with fierce words, barbarously, arrogantly. And then Mongach of the sea raised the strong iron flail, and dealt a blow against the son of the king of the Bretons firmly, vehemently, and the son of the king of the Bretons made a quick leap on high to the left side of the foreigner, and gave him a blow of his sword, so that it went across the joint of his two hands, in such wise, that he cut off the two hands together. And the renowned sharp-shining hero did not stop at them, but he divided the warrior in two right in his midst. And as he fell, an iron apple of the flail with its venomous thorns went into the fair mouth of the son of the king of the Bretons, and took the tongue, and the teeth, and the white bloody clod of the brain out through his backhead behind, so that those two fell together sole against sole, and lip against lip, on that spot.

Then arose the eldest of the children of the king of Norway, and he was intolerable destruction and the spilling of a black deluge, and the filling up of a breach of a hundred, and destruction over the borders, and the wave of overwhelming, and the man that never took a step backward before one or many, to wit, Caisel Clumach, the high-king of Norway himself. For there never came destruction of men, or diminution of people like that into Erinn before, and he had a venomous shield with red flames, which the smith of hell had wrought for him, and if it was put under sea, not one flame of its blaze would be quenched, and he himself was not hotter from it. But when he had taken it upon him, friend or foe did not venture to come near it for the length of his own cast. And he went among the Fianna of Erinn like that, and he did not take any weapon with him, but a sword to defend himself, for not to ply weapons against them did he come, but to let the venom of his shield among them. For the balls of fire that he sent among them, weapon, or dress, or accoutrement could not resist them, but they went through the bodies of the warriors like venomous arrows, so that each man of them would be in a red blaze in the midst of his weapons and his dress, and when somebody else touched him, that blaze seized him; for a splinter of an antediluvial oak-tree, that has been a year in the smoke, would not blaze better than every one of them, as well weapons as dress as accoutrement, and small was every great evil, that ever came into Erinn, compared with that evil.

So then it was Finn said: 'Lift your hands, ye Fianna of Erinn,' said he, 'and give three shouts of blessing to him that will put some delay on the foreigner, so that some of us may escape from him by dint of running.' And the Fianna of Erinn forthwith gave those shouts. A smile then broke upon the foreigner, when he heard those shouts. It was then that Druimderg, the son of Dolar, the son of Dorchaide, the king of the Fianna of Ulster, was near the foreigner, and he had with him a venomous spear, that was in the possession of the Clanna Rudraige one after the other, and the Croderg (the Red-socketed) was its name. And he looked upon the king of Norway, and saw nothing of him without some armour except his mouth, and that wide open as he laughed at the Fianna. Then Druimderg made a cast with the Croderg at him and hit him in his mouth, so that his hideousness was more awful from behind than from before. Then his shield fell down, and its blaze went out as its master fell. And Druimderg went up to him, and separated his head from his body, and boasted of his great deed. And that was the best help the Fianna ever got through the valour of one of the Fianna.

Thereafter those two equally eager and keen armies poured forth against each other, like dense woods, and with their proud noisy strokes, and spilling a black deluge, actively, fiercely, perilously, angrily, furiously, destructively, boldly, vehemently, hastily, and great was there the grating of swords against bones, and the cracking of bones that were crushed, and bodies that were mangled, and eyes that were blinded, and arms that were shortened to the back, and mother without son, and fair wife without mate. Then the beings of the upper regions responded to the battle, telling the evil and the woe that was destined to be done on that day, and the sea chattered telling the losses, and the waves raised a heavy woeful great moan in wailing them, and the beasts howled telling of them in their bestial way, and the rough hills creaked with the danger ofthat attack, and the woods trembled in wailing the heroes, and the grey stones cried from the deeds of the heroes, and the winds sighed telling the high deeds, and the earth trembled in prophesying the heavy slaughter, and the sun was covered with a blue mantle by the cries of the grey hosts, and the clouds were shining black at the time of that hour, and the hounds and whelps, and crows, and the demoniac women of the glenn, and the spectres of the air, and the wolves of the forest howled together from every quarter and every corner round about them, and a demoniacal devilish section of the tempters to evil and wrong kept urging them on against each other.

It was then a hero of the Fianna of Erinn bethought himself that he himself and his family and his kindred had done great evil and wrong to the Clanna Baiscne, and he was desirous to do them good service on that account, and that was Conan the son of Morna. And he quickly moved his hands with his broadsword, and he pierced sides with his dense woundings without quarter, and he cut oft' hands that had been full-valiant, and he destroyed with his good sword people that were fair of face. And to relate his deeds in that encounter were awful.

Now Finn was above the battle there urging on the Fianna, and urging on Conan before all, and the king of the world on the other side urging on the foreigners. Said Finn to Fergus Finnbel: 'Arise to praise Conan for me, so that his courage may be the greater, for good is the slaughter which he deals on my foes.' And

Fergus went up to him. Then heat seized Conan there from the enormity of the fight, and he went outside to let the wind under him. 'That is right, O Conan,' said Fergus Finnbel, 'well doest thou remember the old enmity of the Clanna Morna against the Clanna Baiscne, and thou wouldst fain find death here thyself, if that was ruin to the Clanna Baiscne.' 'For the love of thine honour, O poet, do not revile me without cause, and I will do good work on the foreigners, only let me reach the battle.' 'By my faith, truly,' said Fergus, 'that would be a brave act for thee to do that,' and then he sang a fit of praise for Conan. Conan then went to the battle again, and not worse were his deeds on this occasion. And Fergus Finnbel went where Finn was.

'Who is foremost in the battle now?' said Finn to Fergus. 'Duban, the son of Cas, the son of Cannan,' said Fergus, 'to wit, the son of a warrior of thy people. For he never gives a stroke to any but one stroke only, and none escape alive from that stroke, and three times nine and eighty warriors haven fallen by him until now.' Now, Duban Donn, the son of Nuadu, the son of the king of Cairrge Lethi, the king of Thomond, was on that spot, and this is what he said: 'By our faith, truly, O Fergus,' said he, 'all that witness is true, for there is not in the battle the son of a king, or of a lord, that excels Duban the son of Gas, the son of Cannan, and I will find death there myself, or I will excel him.' And he rushed through the battle with a vehement thundering noise, like the fierce-red blaze of motley flames under a large hill rough with furze, or like a proud wave of overwhelming that beats a sandy white strand. Such was the slaughter and destruction and great carnage he executed among the foreigners, and he made nine rounds through the battle, and killed nine times nine in every round of them. And Finn asked of Fergus:

'Who is foremost in the battle now?' said he. 'Duban Donn, the son of Nuadu, the son of the king of Cairrgi Leithe, the king of Thomond,' said Fergus, 'for nobody has excelled him ever since his seventh year, and nobody excels him now.' 'Rise to praise him,' said Finn to Fergus, 'that his courage may be the greater.' 'Just is it to praise him,' said Fergus, 'for you would think a host was fleeing from or before a heavy drenching of the sea, (the way) the foreigners are running before him on every side.' And Fergus went where Duban Donn was, and began to extol his strength, and his valour and prowess, and to extol his vigour and his arms, and his deeds besides. And he went again where Finn was, and Finn said:

'Who is foremost in the battle now, O Fergus?' said Finn. 'Oscar of the many victories,' said Fergus, 'and he is fighting alone against everybody, for four hundred are standing against him separately, to wit, two hundred Franks, and two hundred of the men of Gairian, and Fiachra Foltlebar, the king of the men of Gairian himself, and all these are beating the shield of Oscar, and no warrior of them has inflicted a wound on him for which he did not give him a wound in return.' 'What is the progress and advance thou seest on Cailte, the son of Ronan?' said Finn. 'He is there without great need after the red slaughter he has made,' said Fergus. 'Go thou to him,' said Finn, 'and tell him to ward off some of the foreigners from Oscar.' Fergus went to him. 'O Cailte,' said he, 'great is the strait yonder in which thou seest thy friend Oscar, under the strokes of the foreigners, and do thou rise to give him some help.'

Cailte went to the place where Oscar and the foreigners were, and he gave a blow of his sword straight in front without sparing to him that was next to him, so that he made two equal portions of him. Oscar raised his head and looked upon him. 'O Cailte,' said he, 'it seems to me, thou hast not ventured to redden thy sword on any one else before overcoming one of those that are opposite my sword. Shame to thee, moreover, all the men of the great world and the Fianna of Erinn in one fight, and thou not able to find combat in it, before thou meddlest in my share of the fight. And I pledge my faith,' said he, 'that I should like thee to be laid low on thy bed of blood on that account.' That altered Cailte's mind and intention, and he set his face again towards the army of the foreigners, with the redness of anger in his countenance, and in his white face, and eighty warriors fell from that onslaught.

Then Oscar went on his slaughterings of very swift course round his own (share of the) fight, and began to close in and to urge and to press the foreigners hard against each other, and he went himself among them after that as a noble roaring river goes over low-stoned, crooked dikes, or like a flock of sheep on a great plain, and a wolf right in their midst driving them together, and not greater is his power over the flock than (that of) Oscar over the foreigners, and not thicker was the sowing of the strand from the men lying low. For whoso came out whole of this battle, he was not one of Oscar's portion, and those four hundred fell by him, and he set his face against the great army again, and went among them like a quickly-roused lion, and began to let loose his anger upon them.

'Who is foremost in the battle now?' said Finn to Fergus. 'Thine own great-spirited son,' said Fergus, 'to wit, Oisin of the many victories, and he is in the thick midst of the foreigners killing them quickly.' 'What aspect is on the fight now?' said Finn to Fergus. 'Woeful is this,' said Fergus, 'for there never came and there never will come any one capable of telling and relating it as it stands now. For I pledge my faith,' said he, 'not closer and not thicker are the dense bush-topped inseparable forests that are densest and most impassable in the west of Europe than they are now. For the bosses (?) of their shields, and the breasts of their hauberks are in each other's hands. And again I pledge my faith,' said Fergus, 'if every second or every third man of those that are in the battle had firebrands in their hands as they strike each other, not more terrible would be the blaze of fire from them on high than the fire that comes out of the rims of their helmets and their battle-hats and their battle-hauberks, from the thin edges of the firm axes and of the sharp-pointed heroes' swords. And again I pledge my faith,' said Fergus, 'it never rained a shower-pouring on a harvest day-heavier than the rain of blood that rains down on the hosts, for the wind, and the stormy groans of the weapons, and the lamenting cries of the hosts threw it upward into the air and the firmament. Again I pledge my faith,'said Fergus, 'no wind that ever came from the elements, tore the like number of leaves from a great forest, that the wind has now torn into the clouds and into the air of long fair-curled golden hair, and of curly jet-black locks, and of long beautiful hairs, that have been cut off by broad, sharp-edged axes. For that blood and locks that rain down on the armies side by side, have smothered them, so that there would not be found in the world anybody who would distinguish any one of them from the other, unless he recognised them by their voices. And many are the warriors striking the shield of Oisin and Oscar, and the warrior whose strait is smallest of the Fianna of Erinn, nine foreigners are striking his shield, and many warriors of them moreover there are, on whom are fifty warriors, or sixty, or eighty, and there are five hundred striking the shield of Oisin and Oscar and Cailte, and great is the strait in which they are above all.'

'Go thou to them, O Fergus,' said Finn, 'and sing a fit of praise to each of them separately, so that their courage and their spirits may be the greater.' Then Fergus went to where Oisin and Oscar and the nobles of the Clann Baiscne were in the very midst of the fight, wounding the heroes and killing and destroying the soldiers, and Fergus began to praise the heroes, and to conjure the warriors, and to urge on the brave, and to extol the champions, and to praise the soldiers, and to exhort the companies, and to command the staying, and to strengthen the resistance, and to urge on the attack, so that he imparted increase of courage and spirit to every man of the Fianna of Erinn, though before that they were of themselves eager and desirous to do bravely. And Fergus went again where Finn was.

'Who is foremost in the battle now?' said Finn to Fergus. 'By my faith, no friend of thine is he who is foremost in it,' said Fergus, 'to wit, the king of the world, to wit, Daire Donn, the son of Loiscenn Lomglunech, and he has come with the swiftness of a swallow or of a hare (?) or of a fawn, or like the gusts of a sharp pure-cold wind coming across the head of a field or the side of a mountain, to seek thee and to find thee out throughout the battle, and he has not left a corner or recess or quarter or flank or front of the battle unsearched for thee. And three times fifty of his henchmen have come with him into the battle as a rear-guard, and two warriors of thy Fianna have seen them, to wit, Cairell Gathbuillech (the Battle-striker) and Aelchinn of Cruachan, and they have encountered the king of the world. For they were not willing to let him to thee, without wounding him, and the rear-guard of the king have fallen by them, but they have not reddened their weapons on him, and they have fallen through him together. And great is the battle-striking of war at him in the midst of the fight coming towards thee.'

Then the king of the world came towards him, and nobody was there near Finn but Daelgus, the son of the king of Greece, and he was called Arcallach of the Black Axe, to wit, he was the first man that brought a broad axe into Erinn, and that was his weapon there. 'I have given my word,' said he, 'that I would never let Finn into the battle or fight before me.' Arcallach rose, and a barbarous blow of the broad axe, that was in his hand, hit the king, so that it cut through the royal diadem and reached the hair, but did not take a drop of blood out of his skin. For the lip of the axe turned, and there went balls of fire over the plain from that blow. And the king of the world gave him a blow and made two equal portions of him.

Then came the illustrious high-king of the world, of noble deeds, strong, robust, proud, powerful, venomous, destructive, nimble, disdainful, full of black crafty thoughts, and the helpful warrior of many clanns, whose is the birthright, the princely, truly-wise Finn, and those two oaks of valour, and the two bears without fear, and the two bears of great deeds, and the two quickly-roused lions went to the place of combat. And the king of the world beheld the venomous sword unsheathed in the hand of Finn, and perceived the venomous battle-strong spear and the knife, and recognised the venomous weapons, by which he was fated to find death. And fear and dread filled him completely, and his comeliness and fair shape left him, and his fingers grew unsteady, and his feet trembled, and his eye and his sight began to squint, when he saw those weapons in the hand of Finn.

Then the two battle-soldiers bared their blue-jointed, iron-smooth, gold-ornamented swords, and attacked each other vehemently, fiercely, closely, madly, and with great blows, with slow feet, actively, strongly, and powerfully, hardily, fiercely, and vehemently, and the high-kings fought a wonderful combat. For they would strike the hearts and heavy clods out of the sides and out of the heart-ribs of each other, and not small was that with which the thunder-feats of those two may be compared, as if it was the rough- breezed gust of a winter-night's wind which, having separated itself equally, would come from east and west against each other, or as if it was the Red Sea fully and equally divided into two sides, striking against each other, or as if it were two days of judgment of fierce deeds, each fighting vehemently for the possession of the earth against the other.

Then he that was never wont to be wounded before that, was greatly weakened in the combat, to wit, the king of the world. For weapons had never been reddened upon him until then. Now, those two battle-soldiers lifted up at the same time their two fearful terrible hands with the blows, and the sword of the king of the world hit the shield of Finn, and took the upper third out of it, and ripped open the hauberk from its girdle downward, and took the breadth of a soldier's hand of flesh and of white skin of his thigh with it to the earth. But the sword of Finn hit the upper shoulder of the shield of the king of the world, so that it split the shield, and broke the sword of the battle-soldier, and the same blow struck the left foot of the king, so that it went into the earth through it. And he gave him the counter-stroke, so that he separated the head and the fair breast from each other. And Finn himself fell in a trance and swoon, and a great number of wounds and cuts and blood-roads of death were on him.

Then Finnachta Fiaclach, to wit, the chief-henchman of the king of the world, seized the diadem of the king, and ran with it to where Conmael, the son of the king of the world, was, and he put the diadem of his father on his head. 'May this be to thee luck of battle and many triumphs, O son,' said Finnachta. And the weapons of the king of the world were given to him, and he went through the midst of the battle to seek Finn. And one hundred and fifty warriors of the Fianna fell by him from that onslaught. Then Goll Garb (the Fierce), the son of the king of

Scotland, saw him and attacked him, and they fought a combat, furious, angry, powerful, close, bold, insupportable, yelling, ready, groanful, sighing, shaft-red, courageous was that combat. Then a blow from the son of the king of Scotland hit that son of the king of the world under the shelter of his shield in his left side, so that it made two equal portions of him.

Finnachta Fiaclach saw that, and again made a rush at the royal diadem, and took it with him to where Ogarmach, the daughter of the king of Greece, was. 'Put on the royal diadem,' said he, 'O Ogarmach, as it is the destiny of the world to be got by a woman, and no nobler woman could get it than thou.' And the king's cry was raised for her on high. 'How am I the better for it?' said Ogarmach,'as there remain not of the Fianna of Erinn any on which I might avenge the death of the king of the world.' And she went to seek Finn in the battle, and Fergus Finnbel saw her and went where Finn was. 'O king of the Fianna,' said he, 'remember the good fighting thou didst against the king of the world just now, and remember thy great and many victories before till this, and great is the need that is coming to thee now, to wit, Ogarmach the daughter of the king of Greece.'

At that the warrior womAn Came towards him. 'O Finn,' said she,'thou art a bad compensation to me for the kings and lords that have fallen by thee and by thy people, and though that is so,' said she, 'thou hast no better compensation for it than thine own self and what remains of thy sons.' 'That is not true,' said Finn, 'and I will lay thine head in its bed of blood like every one's else.' And those two encountered each other like two angry lions, or as if there had arisen to smother each other the bank-overflowing white-foaming curled waves of Clidna, and the long-sided steady wave of Tuaige, and the great right-courageous wave of Rugraide. Such like was the cutting and the striking which those two inflicted on each other, and that was the progress of the combat, though the foolish fighting of the warrior-woman was long, a blow from Finn reached her, and cut through the royal diadem, so that the breast of the hauberk withstood the sword. And he gave a second blow and separated her head and the body from each other. And he fell himself in his bed of blood, and was dead thereafter, but that he rose again.

Now, the hosts of the world and the ñanns of Erinn had fallen side by side there, and none were standing of both armies but the son of Crimthann of the Harbours, to wit, a foster-son of Finn's, and the chief-henchman of the king of the world, to wit, Finnachta Fiaclach. And Finnachta Fiaclach went among the slaughter and lifted up the body of the king of the world with him to his ship, and said: 'Ye Fianna of Erinn,' said he, 'though this battle was bad for the hosts of the great world, it was worse for you; for I shall take possession of the great world in the east and . .. whereas ye have fallen side by side.' Now, Finn heard this, as he lay in his bed of blood, and the nobles of the Clann Baiscne round about him, and he said: 'I am sad that I did not find death, ere I heard the foreigner saying these words, while going back into the great world alive to tell tidings. And nothing avails any deed or feat or victory that I myself or any of the Fianna of Erinn have accomplished, since a man to tell tidings escapes alive of the foreigners. And is there any man alive near me?' 'I am,'said Fergus Finnbel.

'What is the state or slaughter of the battle now?' said Finn. 'Woeful is that, O Finn,' said Fergus, 'I pledge my word that since the armies have mixed in the rout to-day with each other, no foreigner or man of Erinn has taken a step backward before the other, until they have all fallen sole against sole. And I pledge my faith,' said Fergus, 'not visible for the length of sight are the grains of sand or grass on this strand below, owing to the bodies of the heroes and of the battle-soldiers lying low there. And again I pledge my word,' said he, 'there is nobody of the armies that is not on that bloody bed except the chief-henchman of the king of the world and thine own foster-son, to wit, Gael the son of Crimthann of the Ports.' 'Rise to seek him, O Fergus,' said Finn.

Fergus went where Gael was, and asked him how he was. 'Sad is that, O Fergus,' said Gael. 'I pledge my word, that if my hauberk and my helmet were taken off me and all my armour, there would not be a particle of me that would not fall from the other, and I swear, that I am more grieved that yon warrior whom I see should escape alive of the foreigners, than that I myself am as I am. And I leave my blessing with thee, O Fergus,' said Gael, 'and take me on thy back towards the sea, that I may swim after the foreigner, and he will not know the truth, that I am not one of his own people, and .... has reached my life even thus, and I would rejoice if the foreigner fell by me before my soul should depart from my body.'

Fergus lifted him up and took him with him to the sea, and set him swimming after the foreigner. The foreigner waited for him that he might reach the ship, for he thought that he was of his own people. Then Cael raised himself as he swam alongside the ship. The foreigner stretched out his hand towards him. Cael grasped it at the slender wrist, and clasped the firm-clenching inseparable fingers round it, and gave a manly truly-valiant pull at him, so that he drew him out overboard. Then they locked their elegant heroes' hands across one another's bodies and went together to the sand and gravel of the pure sea, and neither of them was ever seen from that time forth.

Then came the ladies and gentlewomen, and the minstrels and gleemen and skilled men of the Fianna of Erinn to search for and to bury the kings and princes of the Fianna, and every one of them that was curable was carried where he might be healed. And Gelges, the daughter of Mac Lugach, to wit, the wife of Gael, the son of Crimthann of the Ports, came, and the weak .... and the truly-woeful sobs that she uttered aloud in seeking her fair mate among the slaughter, were heard over the border of all the land. And as she was there, she saw the crane of the meadow and her two birds, and the wily beast that is called the fox, a-watching of her birds, and when she covered one of the birds to save him, he made a rush at the other bird, so that the crane had to stretch itself out between them both, and so that she would rather have found and suffered death by the wild beast, than that her birds should be killed by him. And Gelges mused on this greatly, and said: 'I wonder not,' said she, 'that I so love my fair lemán, since the little bird is in that distress about his birds.' Then she heard a stag on Druim Ruiglenn above the harbour, and it was bewailing the hind vehemently from one pass to the other. For they had been nine years together and had dwelt in the wood, that was at the foot of the harbour, to wit, Fid Leis, and the hind had been killed by Finn, and the stag was nineteen days without tasting grass, or water, mourning the hind. 'It is no shame for me,' said Gelges, 'to find death from grief for Gael, as the stag is shortening his life for grief of the hind.'

Fergus met her in the midst of the slaughter. 'Hast thou tidings of Gael for me, O Fergus?' said she. 'I have,' said Fergus, 'for he and the chief-henchman of the King of the World, to wit, Finnachta Fiaclach, have drowned each other.' 'Small is the want for me,' said she, 'to bewail Gael and the Clanna Baiscne, for the birds and the waves bewail them strongly.' And then she made the song:

'The high-waved harbour
Of Ruad-Rinn Da Bare sounds:
The drowning of the hero of Loch Da Chonn,
That is what the wave wails against the shore.
.... the crane
In the bog of Druim Da Tren,
She was in great anxiety:
A fox ... was lying in wait for her birds.
Woeful the tune
Which the stag of Druim Leis makes:
Dead is the hind of Druim Silenn,
The stag ... moans after her.
Woeful the song

Which the thrush makes in Druim Chain,
And not less sad the cry
Which the blackbird makes in Leitir Laig.
Sad for me is
The death of the hero that used to lie with me,
The son of the wife from Toire Da Dos
To be ..., round his head.
Woeful the tune
Which the wave of the strand makes against the strand.
Since the stately noble man has died.
Sad for me that Gael did go to meet him.
Sad the strain
Which the wave makes on the strand ...
As for me, my time is at an end,
Worse is my shape ...
Heavy the showers
Which the waves make for him:
As for me, there is no joy for me
Since the ... broke.'
Dead is the swan,
Sorrowful are his birds after him;
Great sorrow gives to me
The grief which has seized the swan.
Gael, the son of Crimthann, is drowned,
There is no treasure for me after him.
Many the lords that fell by his hand,
His shield has sounded.

Then Gelges' soul departed from her body for grief (at the loss) of Gael, the son of Crimthann. And her grave was dug above Ventry, and a stone was raised over her tomb, and her funeral game was celebrated there.

So this is the Battle of Ventry to here,
without addition, without omission.